AGING IN LITERATURE

Edited by

Laurel Porter and Laurence M. Porter

International Book Publishers
5213 Greendale
Troy, Michigan 48098

Laurel and Laurence Porter
Dept. of Romance and Classical Language
Wells Hall
Michigan State University
East Lansing, Michigan 48824-1027

Library of Congress Catalogue Card No. 84-081005
ISBN: 0-936968-08-7

for Myra MacDonald,
Anne E. C. Porter,
Richard and Helen Cline,
and in memory of Fairfield Porter

Table of Contents

Acknowledgments

We would like to thank the editors of *Novel* for permission to republish Chapter 7; of *Soundings*, for permission to republish Chapter 9; and Professor Henri Peyre, and *Laurels*, for permission to reprint "Can Old Be Beautiful? Or Creative? Reflections of an Octogenarian." These articles have been slightly abridged here. We are also grateful to Random House, Inc., for permission to reprint the lines from Mary L. Jackson's "Swinging Down the Avenue" which first appears on page 95 of *I Never Told Anybody: Teaching Poetry Writing in a Nursing Home*, copyright ©1977 by Kenneth Koch; and to William Morrow & Company for permission to reprint the lines from Nikki Giovanni's "Age" which first appeared on pages 44–46 of her *Cotton Candy on A Rainy Day*, copyright ©1978 by Nikki Giovanni.

NOTES on the CONTRIBUTORS and ESSAYS in *AGING IN LITERATURE*

FOREWORD. Overview relating the study of aging to humanistic issues, by Robert N. Butler, M.D. Dr. Butler was the first Director of the National Institute on Aging. He coined the term "ageism" and has written several books and articles, including studies on the use of life review and *Why Survive? Being Old in America,* which won the Pulitzer Prize. He is currently Director of the Department of Geriatrics and Adult Development at the Mt. Sinai Hospital in New York. This is the first such department in the United States.

"Aging and Social Responsibility." An introductory statement linking the essays in this volume to developmental psychology, ethics, and social policy, by Laurel Porter, M.A., M.S.W. Porter is a psychotherapist specializing in intergenerational problems. A former teacher of college literature courses and a Clinical Instructor for the School of Social Work at Michigan State University, she has written on aging and mental health and on social issues in literature.

"Sex and Senescence in Medieval Literature" is a compelling, erudite look at medieval attitudes toward sex in the aged (especially in aged women), by Robert Magnan, who is the author of a doctoral dissertation on aging in the work of the medieval poet Eustache Deschamps.

"Celestina: The Aging Prostitute Witch" by Javier Herrero, Ph.D., examines ageism, misogeny, and witchcraft in the 1499 Spanish play. Herrero is William R. Kenan Professor and Chairman, Department of Spanish, Italian and Portuguese, University of Virginia. He is a former Mellon Professor at the University of Pittsburgh, a Guggenheim and NEH Fellow, and the author of numerous books and articles.

"Montaigne's Final Revisions: An Eriksonian Assessment" by Laurence M. Porter, Ph.D., reveals psychic growth in the late maturity of Montaigne. Porter is Professor of French and Comparative Literature, Michigan State University; a past Visiting Mellon Professor of Comparative Literature, University of Pittsburgh; a Ford Foundation Fellow; member of the Editorial Boards of *Degré Second* and *Nineteenth-Century French Studies;* and the author of a number of books and some fifty articles published in five countries.

"*King Lear* and the Crisis of Retirement," by Laurel Porter, takes a look at Lear's problems in the light of developmental psychology, creating a fresh view of the play.

"Balzac's Myth of Rejuvenation," by Eugene F. Gray, Ph.D., reveals the great novelist's yearning for immortality as betrayed in many works. Gray is Professor and former Chairman, Department of Romance Languages, Michigan State University; a contributor to *The Romantic Movement* since 1973; and the author of studies on Flaubert, Balzac, and medicine and literature.

"Farce and Idealization: Dostoevsky's Ambivalence Toward Aging," by Laurence M. Porter illuminates two opposing trends in Dostoevsky's narrations, where fathers and father figures are either scorned or idealized. Dostoevsky's attitudes evolved, but the great novelist still had unresolved issues on aging when he died in his fifties.

"Proustian Old Age, or the Key to Time Recaptured," by Diana Festa-McCormick, Ph.D., takes us to the final scenes of Proust's monumental novel to illuminate the impact of the narrator's realization of his own aging upon the entire novel. Professor Festa-McCormick, a Guggenheim Fellow (for her work on Proust), is a Professor at Brooklyn College and the author of several books and numerous articles on the novel.

"Life/Death: A Journey (Yasunari Kawabata)," by Bettina Knapp, Ph.D., gives us a rare look at Japanese concepts of aging in the work of the Nobel-prize-winning author, Kawabata. Professor Knapp, who has written more than twenty books, and many articles, is a Guggenheim Fellow, a past President of the Northeast Modern Language Association, and a bearer of the Palmes Académiques. She is a professor at Hunter College and the Graduate Center, CUNY.

"Old Age and the Modern Literary Imagination," by Barbara and Allan Lefcowitz, creates a typology of treatments of old age in English and American literature which will be useful to scholars for years to come. They are Professors of English at the US Naval Academy at Annapolis and Anne Arundel Community College, and are specialists on aging in literature.

CONCLUSION. "Can Old Age Be Beautiful? Or Creative? Remarks of an Octogenarian," by Henri Peyre, concludes the volume. It is a survey of the creativity of great figures in their old age. Professor Peyre is formerly Chairman of French at Yale University and Director of the Graduate Center, CUNY. He is the best-known Professor of French in America, and author of many books and articles.

FOREWORD

By Robert Butler, M.D.

What we have here in this fine volume is a series of contributions related to aging in literature. This collection of essays also reflects the emergence of a new field, "humanistic gerontology." As used in this book, this term signifies the application of research in the humanities to the study of aging; thus, it concerns not only literature but also history, religion, philosophy, and the arts.

It is surprising how few great novels, plays and even films concern so universal and intimate a theme as aging. And when aging is represented in literature it is not always portrayed in a positive manner. But is it really so surprising that aging in literature is touched by ambivalence? After all, although universal and intimate, aging is also progressive and deleterious, and its result is predetermined and well-known. Are great stories made of such predictable processes and outcomes? Is aging, then, so mundane that it cannot attain the stature in the humanities of other great themes of human existence?

I think not. I think its ambivalence and its universality, in fact, indicate its powerful psychological force in the human experience, so powerful that it provokes an incredible amount of denial. As Proust said, old age is one of those realities that we retain the longest as an abstract conception.

The truth is that science has not adequately grappled with aging either. The sciences have only recently come to concern themselves with the fascinating biological mechanisms of aging and to appreciate the underlying genetic, immune, hormonal, cellular and other ingredients of aging.

Frequently the sciences go where the arts have already been. And in some measure that is true with the fields of aging—gerontology and geriatrics—as well. In the beginnings of recorded history, there were certainly "biological" theories about aging and luminous insights that only now modern science and technology can explore. One example is the "wear and tear" theory and its modern counterpart "DNA repair."

This century of old age is breathtaking. It is extraordinary to recognize the grand extension of life of well over 25 years in less than one century. It is remarkable to contemplate further prolongation of life now with death increasingly pushed forward in time and the manifestations of aging held back.

Should we contemplate a new and growing literature related to aging? I think so. It may not be surprising that younger writers have not written about age. But we will see more writers, once old, deal with the themes of age, and we can anticipate older persons turning themselves successfully to literature for the first time in their old age.

I confess that I am surprised by the lack of interest of contemporary professional philosophers in old age and in the recent remarkable developments in gerontology, as defined in the broadest sense as the study of human aging from the biological, social, psychological, ethical and policy perspectives. One might have thought that old age would especially engage the interest of the existential movement. It is certainly clear that we would all gain enormously from the clarification of our thinking and wisdom that comes from writers, philosophers, theologians and artists as they help us to understand what the *good long-lived life* might entail in prospect and in retrospect.

Clinicians and humanists would do well to work together in the everyday world, reviewing and understanding individual lives, to gain insights into characteristics of daily adaptation and survival. Granted, Social Security, Medicare and Medicaid do not reimburse practitioners of "humanistic gerontology" but such a practice of the latter on a grand scale would do much to refine and deepen the meaning of individual and collective lives.

Present-day older people are rather like pioneers. As models, they will help all of us to age better. Their efforts and ours will be enhanced by the contributions of the imagination and human values that we associate with the flourishing of the humanities.

INTRODUCTION

By Laurel Porter

WE USE THE TERM "humanistic gerontology" to signify the application of research in the humanities to the study of aging: literature, history, philosophy, religion, and art as they inform our understanding of human aging. This particular collection of essays is a study of aging, and of values concerning old age, senescence, and death as presented in literature. This meaning of "humanistic" is the same as that used by Walter G. Moss in his essay and annotated bibliography, "Humanistic Perspectives on Aging," which lists literary works dealing with the subject of aging[1]; and by Stuart Picker, Kathleen Woodward, and David Van Tassel in *Aging and the Elderly: Humanistic Perspectives in Gerontology,* a multidisciplinary anthology. In that volume, Richard Freedman argues that there is nothing necessarily "humane" about the humanities. "The greatest literature, indeed, frequently reveals with unblinking truth . . . very negative attitudes toward the elderly."[2] We too have found this true. But to my mind, it is not a question of the humanities being humane, but human, and as such, the definition of a humanistic gerontology as one which is informed by the humanities is consonant with a broader definition of it as a branch of study encouraging special, intimate, searching inquiry into what it means to be human and old.

The seminal, influential article by Robert Butler, "The Life Review: An Interpretation of Reminiscence in the Aged," is an example of humanistic gerontology at its best.[3] An original formulation of therapeutic technique which is greatly enriched by its literary illustrations, it is the single study which most inspired the creation of this collection of essays. In them, distinguished literary critics explore the issues raised by aging, in great works of literature from medieval times to the twentieth century.

One might ask what the study of literature has to offer to the discipline of gerontology. The answer is part and parcel of what the study of literature can offer to the understanding of any human issue. "Literature and literary criticism," as Frederick Wyatt says, "have an immense scope. Together they account for the most comprehensive record for the human condition, both by recreating it in concrete images and by reflecting upon it in reason. . . . Because literature *must* be concerned with human conduct, the literary critic cannot stay only within his formal and aesthetic context. The critic is the only intellectual specialist who still has the freedom to comment on man at large when he comments within his specialty." Theologians, philosophers, and historians might well disagree, but the important point is that the scope of literary endeavor is as broad as that of human endeavor itself, and that "if we want to grasp the actuality of experience, we have to grant absolute relevance to the allusive and metaphoric quality of so much of our thinking, which the language of literature demonstrates with unsurpassed fidelity." At the same time that Wyatt exalts the domain of literary criticism, however, he also attacks it: "It is also hard to understand why the defenders of moral and aesthetic values should prefer a fantasy of human nature to a more realistic grasp of it, even though the psychologist can suggest why the former is so often more comforting."[4]

This question needs to be addressed seriously. The literary critic is interested in the creative artist's vision of human nature—that is, human nature richly depicted, evoking and resembling human reality with more feeling, and thus with more "accuracy" and "realism" than in scientific descriptions. Freud once advised people to "turn to the poets" if they wanted more information about human nature than psychoanalysis could provide. The literary critic is interested, moreover, not only in the artistic production, but also in the act of creating. The critic seeks to understand not only the fictional characters and their environment but also to understand the personality of the implied author (the overarching personality who can be inferred from an entire text, as opposed to the historical author, the province of biographers). For the "fantasy of human nature" is created by human intelligence. The work of art is not imaginary, but imaginative. It is set apart from the reality of other everyday events because it is a human creation. Freud wrote: "Now the writer does the same as the child at play; he creates a world of phantasy which he takes very seriously; that is, he invests it with a great deal of affect, while separating it sharply from reality."[5] Thus each deeply personal literary creation does not derive from popularly-held values alone, but is also shaped by social context, esthetic preference, the constraints of tradition, and the integrity of each author's ideas and personality, which is reflected, among other ways, by his or her choice of literary genre. And by extension, literary criticism differs most significantly from historiography. It studies subjective reflections of the objective.

To the extent that our chapter topics are arranged chronologically, ours could be thought of as an historical—that is, diachronic—volume, tracing the evolution of an attitude. But that would be an error: the more one studies attitudes toward aging throughout history, as reflected in literature and elsewhere, the more one becomes aware of the complex pattern of contrasting values reappearing in every period, a synchronic continuity in which old people are simultaneously feared and revered, cherished and scorned. Our contributors have studied Rojas, Montaigne, Shakespeare, Balzac, Dostoevsky, Proust, and Kawabata, and, in overviews, many others. We have imposed no topics, and no editorial bias upon them. To present our point of view, we have made brief introductory comments to each chapter, signaling some of their broader implications. The last two essays, and Professor Gray's, are prefaced by Laurence Porter. The other prefaces are mine.

This is, then, a volume of literary criticism, but treating a topic of social significance. Speaking now as a social worker, I would like to make a few remarks on current psychosocial issues in gerontology: developmental psychology; social policy; and cultural relativism. These issues of necessity concern not only the elderly, but also their families, public and institutional responsibility, and societal values.

As editors, we have constantly in mind the concepts of developmental psychology, particularly those of Erik Homburger Erikson. In *Identity and the Life Cycle: Selected Papers,*[6] this celebrated psychoanalyst and psycho-historian postulates a series of tasks faced each in turn throughout the life cycle. Each stage offers a choice between a stagnant and a self-actualizing stance. The final stage involves the struggle between ego integrity and despair. The old person who achieves integrity accepts her or his own life as something which had to be, without deep regrets or longing for it to have been different. The stage preceding integrity, however, called by Erikson "generativity" and extending from full maturity until old age, is the one to which we shall allude most frequently. Learning how to take care of other people and things, and developing a concern for future generations, marks this stage in human development. In order to be able to care about posterity, one must first have developed a healthy sense of identity and autonomy; to care for children, one must have relinquished dependence on one's parents.

Personal identity, however, is not something concrete which may be earned and then hoarded. According to Erikson, a sense of identity, described as "knowing where you're going," can be periodically lost and regained, like a good conscience.[7] In this view, emotional growth arises from the increased sense of identity accrued at the conclusion of each stage of life, or crisis, encountered.

The Eriksonian stages to which we refer are not static, nor does he present them as such. But labelling them separately does help focus attention upon important maturational tasks. As opposed to other psychological models, the advantages of a developmental perspective are that it is growth-oriented; it devotes some attention to aging and to old age; it does not necessarily look for pathology; and it usually does not differentiate invidiously between sexes, unlike Freud ("anatomy is destiny"; "penis envy"; "what does a woman want?"). Developmental perspectives have wide applicability. They can be used to understand cognitive growth; to analyze observational learning; to study social cognition, physical growth, language acquisition, and psychosexual maturation (where Freud is limited to the last of these four areas); and most importantly for our study, developmental psychology—unlike the operant conditioning framework in its most radical forms[8]—is applicable to complex human behavior. Developmental theories should themselves be used flexibly. We must keep in mind that different people, indeed different peoples, change at different ages and not in every instance with the orderliness implied by developmental schemes.

"Identity crises" are not confined to adolescents, developmental psychology tells us. Many an adult has never completed the childhood and adolescent tasks of separating from the parents. If the adult child has not individuated from the elderly parents, problems will arise in this phase of life just as in every other stage. A typical example is the middle-aged couple who comes to treatment for marital problems related to their responsibilities toward elderly parents. The husband, for example, insists that the wife take care of his folks; the wife wants to return to school for an advanced degree. The clinical summary of the problem runs as follows: "In the course of therapy, it became evident that this man had never truly separated from his parents, still was in terror of his father and needed to be the 'good child' as he had always been. Only when this stance began to interfere with his own marriage—his wife had become increasingly depressed and angry at having to take care of her in-laws—was he ready to work through some of his earlier feelings. . . ."[9]

I am not suggesting that adult children abandon their aged parents. On the contrary, they will be able to help them more effectively—and with less strain on their own lives, marriages, and children—if they possess a clear sense of who they are and of what they need apart from and alongside of their parents' identity and needs. Many people feel guiltily that they are not "doing enough" for their folks, that they will *never* be able to do enough. While instances of blatant negligence, ingratitude, and abuse exist, and according to some indicators may be on the rise, the fact is that most families go the limit for their aged parents.[10]

There are lots of ways in which we feel, these days, that we have disappointed, betrayed or abandoned our elderly. A response even less constructive, perhaps, than sterile self-castigation is to project our guilt upon something outside ourselves. Literature and the media make convenient scapegoats, as if they had a demonic will of their own, independent of the wishes of society. One social commentator came up with the preposterous suggestion that "the reading of poetry, a sensitizing experience, serves to reinforce negative stereotypes" regarding aging, and should therefore perhaps be avoided because of the presence of "strongly negative attitudes about physical, emotional, social losses" in old age. Many others complain, for example, about the portrayal of old people on television. In reality, TV elders, although underrepresented, are usually portrayed as rather wise and gentle. In contrast to their middle-aged children, who seem viciously competitive, they often come off as witty, agile, outspoken, clever, appealing, and good with children. Studies of aging in film also show that certain positive types are current. Some older movie characters adventurously seek a new life, like the hero of "Harry and Tonto" played by Art Carney; others boisterously live in the present, to the fullest, until it no longer makes sense to do so, like the Ruth Gordon heroine of "Harold and Maude." A typology of aged characters in modern literature can be found in Chapter Nine of this book. Some are good, some are bad. The arts mirror society and its values; they do not direct them.

What then should we do about the elderly? Surely it is important for all of us adults to examine our individual responsibilities, and to carry them out as best as we can. But let us not overlook our collective responsibilities in the process. There are reasons for concern. For the ways in which we as a society have been letting old people down—and we have—are far more devastating than any damage we may do individually. In this perspective, I see two major social issues. One is the fact that current American social policy *encourages* commitment to nursing homes. Alternatives to institutionalization are not paid for by the government, but long-term institutionalization is. The second issue belongs to a separate realm of social work endeavor, and yet is oddly related: it concerns the way in which we dehumanize old people. I'll briefly examine both issues here.

Medicaid covers the cost of long-term care but *not* at-home care, day care, or outpatient services for the elderly at community mental health centers or family service agencies. While most Americans would argue that institutionalization should be a last resort, social policy in this country makes it by far the easiest, and sometimes the only, possibility. Families are tortured with guilt for having committed their elders to nursing homes. Yet in most cases they truly cannot afford, cannot possibly manage, to do other wise. And when an old person is discharged from the hospital after, say, a fall or a stroke or a heart attack, it is commonplace for a family to be pressured into sending the old person straight to a nursing facility. The hospital's *urgent priority* is to discharge patients as soon as possible, and yet the older patient's health problems typically resolve themselves slowly or not at all. It would be extremely difficult for the overburdened nuclear family to nurse Mom or Dad back to health at home. The doctor and the social worker are giving the best advice they can in the circumstance: commit. And for this type of nursing care and this type only, Medicaid will pay. Moreover, a large proportion of the aged are "placed" upon their doctor's recommendation because of apparent psychiatric symptoms—in particular, disorientation, which in many cases is actually due not to senility but to treatable chemical imbalances which have gone undetected, or to reversible effects of the trauma of illness and of hospitalization itself. New policies on Hospice care are a positive development which will encourage at-home care.

A keen awareness of our individual values is necessary before we can act collectively to effect sweeping changes in politics and policy. So the contribution which may be made by humanistic thought to the challenges of an aging population is not ancillary, theoretical, or superfluous. But a heightened individual sense of humanistic values does not suffice to create social change. For that, political action is necessary.

The second social issue I'd like to explore has to do with the devaluation of old people in our society. I. A. Richards wrote that "man is not a thing to be pushed about, however kindly or beneficently . . . The humanities pin a faith . . . on the ideal autonomy of the individual man."[11] This humanistic faith, by the way, is a core element of the social worker's code of ethics. Yet the values of individual dignity, autonomy, and self-determination very often disappear when it comes down to individual elderly cases. The dehumanization of the old often betrays itself when people treat them like infants. "Old men are as babes again," said King Lear's unkind daughter. But *no* adult, no matter how weak, disoriented, or helpless, can *ever* be a child again. Those who have lived longer than we should never be treated as if those years had not elapsed, as if they had not reached adulthood. Activity programs in institutions for the aged tend to drift to the opposite extremes of denying the fact of aging—old people won't be or seem old if they are encouraged to act middle-aged—and of pushing old people into trivial activities like weaving pot-holders or lap-warmers, on the grounds that since they are disengaging from life, it doesn't much matter what they do so long as you keep their hands busy. Such trivialization is more widespread, and probably far more harmful, than outright disrespect.

It's hard to see clearly how the old are treated, and what such treatment means, because our attitudes about aging are terribly confused. We learn that nursing homes often are run in scandalous fashion, and we feel outraged. We feel guilty when we see someone neglected or impoverished or diminished because of old age. But we are also overcome with the fear of growing old ourselves; and the most common and least effective reaction to this fear is a strategy of avoidance. The very young report that they would rather die than to become old or ugly or ill. But the more human contact we have with the aged, the more love and respect we can feel for these morally strong, often courageous versions of ourselves who have seen more, understood more, and done more than we. Old people do not infantilize each other the way their juniors infantilize them. They have learned solidarity. When the city bus jerks to a halt and an old woman falls down, the driver is apologetic. The young passengers look concerned, horrified, pitying, or embarrassed. But the other *old people* on the bus help her to her feet, offer her their seats and exchange steady looks. In a network of mutual communication, they make fists to each other which clearly signify: "We must hang on tighter to the bars, to precent such falls."

The old person has often become free of the petty pridefulness of earlier years. Her vulnerable human condition has been laid bare in ways she can't ignore. "I've got cancer of the mouth," an old woman confides to another in the park. "How does it look?" the stranger asks. "I might make it," is the reply. And the other nods: "Hang on!" Solidarity and endurance.

Trivialization is one form of devaluing the old. The uncritical acceptance of stereotypes concerning them is another. It is not well known that old people in general have not turned away from the world. They vote more than any other group except the healthy middle-aged. Nor are they, as some believe, politically conservative across the board. They do not vote in blocs, but in a varied way, like other people. They *are* like other people, with the full range of individual differences of belief, background, and opinion that everyone else has. Life has not allowed them to be so rigid as people sometimes imagine them. Old people have had to adjust to the Depression, World Wars, space travel. They've seen a lot: they're not shocked as easily as we might think. They are sensuous. They still delight to move, to sing, and to make love. When Kenneth Koch taught poetry writing in a New York City nursing home, he played jazz to inspire them. And Mary L. Jackson, age 93, wrote:

> Swinging down the avenue
> Dancing, curving
> With all them cats looking at me
> Hollering "Do it, Miss Mary, do it!"
> Curving with all of them cats on my trail.[12]

How often are we surprised by such a gift, and such a zest for life in one so old!

But the most pernicious dismissal of all is a medical plague:

the overprescription of drugs for the aged. Ageism in the mental health establishment has been noted by many skilled observers.[13] Unfortunately indeed, some of the mental health problems and disorientation experienced by aged persons are avoidable, and iatrogenic. Careless prescription, interactive prescription, and overprescription can be responsible for many complaints in elders. The abuse of sedatives contributes seriously to perceived "senility" and confusion in nursing homes.[14] In general, medical researchers have not yet bothered to pin down the ways in which an old person's metabolism responds to drugs more slowly, but in smaller doses, than does the body of a younger person. Drug prescription abuse is merely one symptom of ageism in medicine, in mental health, and in society at large. Treatment approaches other than drug therapy should be more widely tested and explored. These include social therapy (developing and maintaining interpersonal and social skills); ergotherapy (work); ludotherapy (play and games); kinesitherapy (exercise); and psychotherapy.[15] Once drugs are discontined, it sometimes becomes obvious that the patient was not suffering from chronic brain syndrome at all, but rather from an acute shock or grief reaction.[16]

Societal dismissal of the aged outside of nursing homes is less dramatic, but equally telling. Retirement parties, for instance, are perfunctory. Not that our society is alone in giving short shrift to the rites of passage in later life. In van Gennep's classic study, adults rites of passage jump from "betrothals and marriage" to "funerals." As he puts it,

> There do not seem to be any rites of menopause, or of the graying of hair, although both these mark the beginning of a new phase of life which is very important among the semicivilized. In general, either old women become identified with men and therefore participate in their ceremonies, political activities, and so forth, or they acquire a special position within their own sex group, especially as ceremonial leaders. Old age brings increased social standing for the men.[17]

Thus even in societies where old age is dignified, there is no particular celebration for entering into it. Peter Stearns has written that "sociological gerontology abounds with introductions concerning the declining place of old people in modern society, displaced from the patriarchal eminence of the respectful village. . . . But it is an unexamined hypothesis, designed mainly to create a lachrymose atmosphere and gaining credence by repetition alone."[18] I wouldn't want to be guilty of such a thing. The essays in this volume should dispel any notion that a golden age of veneration once existed for the aged, I think, quite as well as any historical study could do.

In any event, the question of how people treat other people is always more complex than simple linear comparisons, lachrymose or not, can convey. Cross-cultural data point this out. Among the Abkhasians of the U.S.S.R., for instance, everyone is aware of her or his place in a more or less stifling (at least it would be so for me), rigid hierarchy based upon age and sex. People get to live very long in Abkhasia—you have seen them in the Dannon yoghurt commercials—but with a lifestyle which many Americans, especially women, would find intolerable. No one dares step out of expected roles. But there are tradeoffs. People are not fatalistic about the death of the old, and freely express grief when even the oldest die. In Abkhasia it is more advantageous to be male than to be female—as it is in our society—but it also is more advantageous to be old than to be young. That society, with its certainty about where each member belongs, in many ways has great appeal.[19]

A more cosmic and fluid, although equally traditional view of the older person's identity as part of a comprehensive scheme, is found in Lao-tzu's poem, "Tao te ching."

> To know men is to be wise;
> To know one's self is to be illumined.
> To conquer men is to have strength:
> To conquer one's self is to be stronger still,
> And to know when you have enough is to be rich.
> For vigorous action may bring a man what he is determined to have,
> But to keep one's place [in the order of the universe] is to endure;
> And to die and not be lost, this is the real blessing of long life.[20]

Attitudes toward aging are as diverse as the peoples of the earth. When Claude Lévi-Strauss studied the Brazilian Indians, he found linguistic evidence of attitudes far harsher than our own: "The Nambikwara have only one word for 'pretty' and 'young,' and another for 'ugly' and 'old'."[21]

But whatever may be the biases of societies, primitive or cultured, present or past, our joylessness regarding aging in general and retirement in particular have a great deal to do with the overvaluation of productivity. In a poem entitled "Age," Nikki Giovanni writes:

> there are so many too many
> who have never worked
> and therefore for whom death
> is a constant companion
> as lack of marriage
> lowers divorce rates
> lack of life
> prevents death
> the unwillingness to try
> is worse than failure
> . . . .
> it may simply be that work
> is so indelibly tied
> to age that the loss
> of work brings the depression
> of impending death[22]

As I have tried to suggest, great literature and popular culture both mirror our values. But literature also communicates the personal meditations of original and insightful minds. It is not basically didactic, but esthetic. No one *learns* stereotypes from literature, although a limited reading list can reinforce sterotypes. On the contrary, a wide-ranging encounter with works of art invites us in many ways to reflect upon the meaning of human experience. In this volume, the focus is on human aging, an experience most of us will have. Literary masterpieces can contribute in making our mental images of aging to be at once more immediate, more finely-drawn, more imaginative, more poignant. In the end our lives will be better for having seen life's later years with a slightly keener eye.

1

SEX AND SENESCENCE IN MEDIEVAL LITERATURE

By Robert Magnan

[Robert Magnan exposes ageism and sexism spanning several centuries of European literature. The old were scorned and their sexuality was reviled. This was particularly true for women. The Christianity of the time was sexually repressive—and we must remember that medieval literature is a Christian literature. "As far as the history of sex is concerned, the record of the early Christian Church was a formidable one. Other Western societies had condemned, with varying degrees of severity, adultery (usually), contraception (rarely), abortion (sometimes), homosexuality (sometimes), infanticide (rarely), and masturbation (rarely). The Church proscribed them all."[1] Sex was associated with sin and guilt in the medieval mind immeasurably more than it is today. As a result of moral repression, attitudes toward sexuality within this tradition—ours—were both puritanical and prurient. Sexual repression was far greater for the old, partly because of the dogma that intercourse should serve only for reproductive purposes and partly because of the cult of youth and beauty in courtly love. Among medieval authors, the verdict is virtually unanimous in rejecting the sexuality of the aged. This basic agreement among writers from different centuries and different nations suggests that social norms are accurately reflected here.

Only in very recent years have attitudes toward sex among the aged begun to change. Witness the following statements from popular French pamphlets: "1807: 'Abuses of the hymen harm even the most robust people.' 1873: 'Like our hair, our desires should wither.' 1911: 'Each sacrifice to Venus is, for the old man, a spadeful of earth on his head.' 1931: No more sex after 60 or 65; 'the genital secretions should remain to the profit of the organism that produces them.' "[2] The tragedy is that many old people faithfully followed such advice, abstaining for the good of their health.

The double standard regarding the aging of the two sexes lingered far beyond the Middle Ages. Men might lament the infirmities of advanced age, but women were believed to age and to wrinkle earlier than men, losing their sexual desirability sometime in early middle age. Think of the advice of Anne de France (1460–1522), cited below: "As soon as a woman reaches 40, whatever beauty she may have had, it is obvious that not even the best designed clothing can conceal the wrinkles on her face." Then compare this remark in a nineteenth-century article on cosmetics: [once a woman has reached the age of fifty] "there is no hope, no way to repair the irreparable outrage of the years."[3] Granted, Anne de France's hapless advisee is ten years younger than her unfortunate Victorian counterpart, but the underlying assumption is identical: only young women are attractive. Such attitudes persist in the twentieth century, although some changes began after the sexual revolution of the 1960s. By the 1970s, enlightened, healthy advice to old people about continuing their sex lives was just beginning to be published.[4] The underlying biases have by no means disappeared—Eds.]

GUILLAUME DE LORRIS begins *The Romance of the Rose*, "Where all of the Art of Love is enclosed," with a description of the various qualities that prevent entry into the Garden of Delight, the *locus amoenus* (pleasant spot) of love. Among the portraits of the enemies of love found on the wall is Old Age, a condition considered worse than death.[1] This most influential work is not the only piece of medieval literature where Age is set in opposition to Love and Love is for Youth alone; expressions of this attitude abound. This study proposes to examine the relationship between sexuality and aging in various writings of the Middle Ages in Western Europe. What were the prevailing attitudes toward the process of aging and what is the medieval mythology of sexual senescence?

Medieval Life Span

Our traditional tendency is to assess aging not only in terms of actual changes in the individual (aging as the entire course of life, from birth), but rather more in terms of generalized expectations (aging as the approach toward a probable time of death). It sems worthwhile, then, to consider some estimates of the medieval life span.

Unfortunately, demographic data are limited. According to J. C. Russell, the most reliable information comes from England after the middle of the thirteenth century.[2] Longevity was significantly less than it is today, ranging between 17 and 35 years for the period from 1276 to 1450. Out of 1000 people born during this period, an average of 350 reached age 40, 200 or so reached 50, perhaps 90 attained age 65, and a dozen would live to be 80 or older.[3] Similar figures are reported for Italy from 1200 to 1430.[4] These figures suggest a rough profile of the demography of aging in medieval European literature.

The fundamental authority on the length of life was the Bible, Psalm 89/90.10, which sets threescore years and ten as the normal limit, with the possibility of attaining fourscore. These figures were accepted by most writers.[5] Around 1265, Philippe de Novare wrote that octogenarians ought to desire death even if they could live longer.[6] Dante suggests that it is almost impious to live past 80: had Jesus not been crucified, He would have been changed from a mortal body to an immortal one in his eighty-first year.[7]

Divisions of Life

Life was not only measured, but divided. The medieval mind took seriously the Book of Wisdom 11:20–21—"You have ordered all things in measure and number and weight." Philippe Ariès summarizes the situation neatly:

> The 'ages of life' occupy a considerable place in the pseudo-scientific treatises of the Middle Ages. It is hard for us today to appreciate the importance which the concept of the 'ages' had in ancient representations of the world. A man's 'age' was a scientific category of the same order as weight or speed for our contemporaries; it formed part of a system of physical description and explanation which went back to the Ionian philosophers of the sixth century B.C., which medieval compilers revived in the writings of the Byzantine Empire and which was still inspiring the first printed books of scientific vulgarization in the sixteenth century. (. . .) The popularity of the 'ages of life' made the theme one of the most common in profane iconography.[8]

Two features are of particular interest here. First, in many of these systems the onset of senescence is placed between ages 40 and 50, and some writers consider it to come even earlier. Augustine seems to be exaggerating little, if at all, when he claims that "the most learned authorities of this world define the age of human maturity as being about thirty years; they say that after that period a man begins to go downhill towards middle age and senility."[9] Nine centuries later, Dante summarizes a common belief that the course of life is similar to the celestial arc, rising to its zenith between ages 30 and 40, midway through the threescore and ten or fourscore years of life; as evidence, he points out that Jesus died in His thirty-fourth year, as it was not proper for Him to experience the decline of life.[10] The second feature of interest is that the Chain of Aging is generally considered to consist of two parts.[11] Although there are very precise systems of dividing life into a number of stages, what we find most often in medieval European literature is simply the dichotomy of *juventus* and *senectus*.

For this reduction and polarization of the Chain of Aging, there is ample support to be found in the phenomena underlying the various philosophical divisions. In the four-part continuum of the qualities of heat and moisture, there is a natural separation at the point where heat, the vital force in the Greek tradition, is lost, marking the end of youth and the beginning of old age. Similarly, distinctions made between the denominations of melancholy (cold and dry) and of phlegm (cold and moist) blur, and senescence is associated in the medieval mind with a dual dominance.[12] Jupiter, believed to rule over the content period of mature age, tends to be eclipsed by Saturn, an influence in which there is nothing good—he is cold, dry, heavy, slow, dark, avaricious, and deprived of sex.[13] The influence of Mars, believed to be dominant during the period of life which might now be called early middle age, is extended and weakened, no doubt in part by the legends of epic warriors of advanced age, such as the septuagenarian Beowulf and the 200-year-old Charlemagne; and when the interests of society shift from war to love, Venus quite naturally assumes a far greater importance, as an influence more characteristic of *juventus*.[14] Thus, although there may be in principle seven planetary influences over the course of life, a dichotomous system prevails, with the two dominant influences Venus and Saturn, the two ages *juventus* and *senectus*, in conflict. Finally, those who compare the life span to the cycle of the four seasons distinguish between the productive period of the year and the time after harvest, the cold and barren months of winter.

The result of this reduction of the various divisions of life is summarized by Philippa Tristram: "When the Ages are reduced to two, they become opposed voices in a debate which can reach no conclusion; they are the vexed polarities of a mutable world."[15] This dichotomy of *juventus* and *senectus*, these "vexed polarities," invite comparison with dichotomies of other natural and supernatural phenomena, such as day and night, light and dark, and good and evil, as well as life and death. Regardless, then, of the stages of life established in philosophical writings, the natural continuum of physiological and psychological changes of life polarizes around these two contrasts—idealized Youth, the best of *juventus*, characterized by health, productivity, and joy; and idealized Age, the worst of *senectus*, a period of infirmity, uselessness, and misery.

Polarization of Sexuality

Senescence, the passage from *juventus* into *senectus*, involves, among other changes, a change in sexuality. We are not concerned here with actual physiological and psychological aspects of senescence, but rather with the significance of sexuality in the medieval mythology of aging. With the efflorescence of interest in physical love in the twelfth century and the development of the courtly love ethic, as well as the increase in emphasis placed on the concept of *contemptus mundi,* sexuality assumed a preponderant importance in the *juventus-senectus* dichotomy.

Briefly stated, the concept of courtly love developed from a confluence of several currents. Sexual passion was rendered less dangerously physical and more elaborate through a process of sublimation drawing upon the Christian feudal framework, as a compromise of natural urges and social restraints. Sexuality was ennobled under the influences of the classical ideal of *amicitia* (friendship), Christian *caritas* (disinterested love), and the feudal bonds of fealty and service. Such sublimation both idealizes sexuality and extends its influence. This elaboration of love, which we find codified to varying degrees, had several important effects: it occupied the leisure time and energies of the aristocracy, it distinguished those who showed senstivity to this sublime concept in words or in deeds, and it enhanced the meaning of erotic activity.

Courtly love sublimated sexuality, but this sublimation, in following Christian and feudal lines, formed an elite society in conflict with the larger social and moral structure. In considering love more noble if given freely, this ethic promoted extramarital sexual relationships; but adultery was wrong, of course, from both Christian and feudal perspectives, since marriage was a bond fundamental to moral, social, and political stability. There was also a conflict, in principle at least, between social power and political power: central to both was a feudal bond of homage, but whereas political homage was rendered to a lord, social homage was to a lady. This system of love promoted idolatry: women as sexual beings, all descendants of the temptress Eve, were elevated to the position of respect traditionally accorded to only the spiritual ideal, Mary; and in effect the source of Christian sin became the source of courtly salvation. Finally, however idealized and sublimated, the basic force beneath courtly love was always sexuality.

What we consider courtly love, then, embodied a tension

between physical interests and spiritual values, between natural urges and social restraints. This tension found an expedient resolution in the split between *juventus* and *senectus*. If the courtly love ethic allowed the physical and emotional forces of human nature to transgress the basic spiritual and social limits, there was necessarily a compensation in respect. As the Fathers of the Church had legitimized what they borrowed from pagan culture by establishing a duality of interpretation—"good sense" and "bad sense"—so in developing courtly love, in ennobling physical love depreciated by Christian tradition, society and literature necessarily distinguished a proper sexuality, associated with youth, and an improper sexuality which was to be condemned, the sexuality of senescence.

This distinction fit naturally with the dichotomy of *juventus* and *senectus*. *Juventus* was a time of folly, of idleness, of passions and pleasures, hot and moist, sanguine, under the influence of Venus. *Senectus,* in contrast, was a time of reason, of gravity and repentance, of social and moral responsibility, cold and generally dry, melancholy and phlegmatic, under the influence of Saturn. Thus the conflict between the courtly celebration of physical love and the traditional Christian morality, with its emphasis on contempt for things worldly and its misogyny, was resolved, or at least lessened, through the distinction between *juventus* and *senectus*. If love is natural and right for *juventus,* it is necessarily unnatural and wrong for *senectus*. If the world of the flesh is to be viewed with contempt, this is considered appropriate in old age, but not in youth.[16] The *locus amoenus* of courtly works is a Garden of Eden, where sexual love is noble, free from evil. It is time that makes sexuality evil: senescence is a fall from courtly ideality into Christian morality. In the passage from *juventus* to *senectus,* man and woman follow the path of Adam and Eve, physical love becomes shameful, and the only good love thereafter is the love of God.[17]

Sexual Double Standard

Medieval European works generally hold that women age earlier than men. The primary reason for this difference was that a woman's value, both sexually and generally, depended far more upon physical beauty than did a man's. La Belle

Heaulmière described the situation of virtually all women when she recalled in later years the "high command that Beauty had ordained for me over clerks, merchants, and churchmen."[18] Women's social influence derived from their beauty, which was prized and idealized in courtly circles. We find ample evidence of this not only in countless descriptions of young and beautiful women, but also in detailed portraits of ugly older women.

Appearances were considered far less important in the sexual senescence of men; here the primary indication of decline was graying or white hair. Its significance as an emblem marking the onset of senescence was succinctly stated by John Gower's *Confessio Amantis* (ca. 1385). Venus rejects the would-be Lover, saying:

> There is no delight
> That I may find in you;
> For love's delight and hoary locks
> Never make good bedfellows.[19]

In an anonymous fifteenth-century poem, a young woman married to an older man longs for a lively lover 30 years old, an age which Deschamps considers ideal.[20] There is much evidence that the prime age for women was thought to be a virginal youth between 15 and 20. In portraying a beautiful woman, Deschamps states that

> The May rose is 15 or 16 years old:
> That is the perfect time of flourishing youth.[21]

The conventional ideal of feminine beauty in medieval literature and art favors slender figures and small breasts.

Many writers locate the passage from *juventus* into *senectus* much earlier in women than age 60. Deschamps expresses the prevailing attitude when he describes a woman lamenting the loss of her youth: "Honored by many a man until age 20/[. . .]/ Everyone abandoned me before 30."[22] "Young bloom" is the desideratum expressed with crude forthrightness by Januarie in Chaucer's "Merchant's Tale." He wants to marry at age 60:

> I absolutely refuse to have an old wife;
> She shall not be older than 20, for certain.
> I prefer to have old fish and young flesh:

. . . .
I want no woman of 30:
That is nothing but bean-straw and fodder.[23]

By 40 the years have definitely taken their toll on women. We find Anne de France advising her daughter, "As soon as a woman reaches 40, whatever beauty she may have had, it is obvious that not even the best designed clothing can conceal the wrinkles on her face."[24] Shakespeare will later use this age as a milestone in Sonnet II:

When forty winters shall besiege thy brow,
And dig deep trenches in thy beauty's field,
Thy youth's proud livery, so gazed on now,
Will be a tatter'd weed, of small worth held.

The damage of time is undeniable at 40: a woman can no longer hide her age, and her beauty is of little value.

Since men are considered to age later than women, we find poignant situations reflecting a major shift in the business of love. In a poem by Conon de Béthune (late 12th C.), a woman no longer "at her greatest worth" deigns at last to welcome a suitor whose advances she had long rejected, only to find that the years have reversed the advantage that she once enjoyed; he finds her "quite pale and changed in color" and he declines.[25] In a somewhat similar situation described in a fifteenth-century poem, an older man accepts the advances of an older woman; but then, suddenly changing his mind, he points out, "Lady, my hair may be gray,/But your belly is wrinkled;/I may be old, but you are worn out."[26]

A general pattern of sexual senescence emerges from these works: a woman peaks in worth between 15 and 20, sometimes even earlier, then declines gradually until around 30, an age which typically marks the end of *juventus;* a man enjoys a plateau in worth from 15 or 20 to around 35 or 40, with a less marked decline into *senectus*. Yet most medieval writers do not attempt to deal with the problematic, hazy area of the first signs of aging; rather, they describe more advanced stages, an established or extreme *senectus*. To appreciate more fully these descriptions, it is necessary to consider them within the rhetorical tradition.

Influence of Rhetorical Tradition

Horace advises writers in his *Ars Poetica:* "You must observe the characteristics of each age and assign a fitting grace to natures that shift with the years. [. . .] Many are the discomforts of age [. . .]. The years as they come bring many blessings: many do they take as they go. [. . .] We shall do wisely to dwell on the attributes proper to each period of life."[27] Medieval authors followed this advice, but with the simplicity of perspective expressed by Juvenal—"Young people vary a lot [. . .], but the old are all alike."[28] When Aristotle became known in the West, his *Rhetoric* added weight to this tradition of contrasting *juventus* and *senectus,* stating that "older men and those who have passed their prime have in most cases characters opposite to those of the young," and describing the psychology and behavior of this third age in some detail, quite negatively.[29]

Horace, Juvenal, and other classical authors served as sources of negative characteristics for *senectus.*[30] Medieval rhetorical treatises continue this tradition of distinguishing a period of infirmity, ugliness, ill humor, and misery. A treatise written about 1270 gives striking advice about characterizing *juventus* and *senectus:*

> *May the youth be cheerful, may he stroll through pleasant woods,*
> *May he be of changing voice, and may he delight in games.*
> *He ought to be audacious, carried away by love,*
> *Nor should he fear darkness, but rather go about in darkness.*
> *May the old character be shameful, and may he be far from*
> *Tranquil, and may he desire everything that he sees.*
> *May the old man be desirous, boastful, slow, and greedy,*
> *And may he deny his riches: he has possessions, and he lacks them.*[31]

Geoffrey of Vinsauf, in his *Poetria Nova* (ca. 1208–1213), advises how to describe people by associating their physical and mental features with conventional contrasts between *juventus* and *senectus,* by painting in stark black and white.[32] Building on the foundations on such rhetorical authorities, classical and medieval, with material borrowed from a growing number of sources, writers developed their portraits of senescence and old age.

The most developed early description is to be found in the six elegies attributed to Maximianus (middle 6th C.), a series of dismal laments. In the first elegy there is a reference to the characteristics of old age as the "first fruits of death."[33] As in many medieval works, there is little or no difference between descriptions of aging and lists of the signs of death.[34] Another influential treatment of aging is to be found in the *De Miseria* of Innocent III. He lists the problems of aging with "lugubrious lyricism,"[35] using rhyme and rhythm to make his pathetic description all the more memorable. Antonio Pucci begins his "Canzone della Vecchiezza" (ca. 1375) with a line reminiscent of Horace—

> Old age comes to man, when it comes,
> With every suffering and every deficiency—

and then he devotes some 130 lines to detailing these sufferings and deficiencies.[36] Among the various poems by Deschamps dealing with aging, the best known is the ballad beginning, "Je deviens courbes et bossus," which lists the characteristics of a man of 60: his cold, thin, dry body is bent, with a humped back, pains in his chest, and limbs trembling; he is unable to walk without assistance; he is hard of hearing; his nose is runny; his hair is white and thinning; his teeth are weak, long, pointed, and yellow, and they smell like bilge water; he is usually asleep or dozing off; he has little appetite, preferring only to drink; he is impatient, covetous, miserly, jealous of the pleasures of others, suspicious, easily angered, nostalgic, talkative, and quick to blame the young. This list is punctuated by the blunt refrain, "These are the signs of death."[37]

Two features are common throughout these works. Aging is usually not depicted as a long process, a series of gradual changes, but rather as a generally sudden and distinct stage of life, a time at which one's thoughts turn away from the world and toward death, either simply as an escape from the growing misfortunes of life or also as a beginning of eternal life. These descriptions tend to be lists of stock characteristics, with apparently little effort made to assess the actual, individual process of senescence.

Interest in allegory encouraged representation of the life process in terms of personifications of Youth and Age, always in contrast. This further simplifies and dramatizes the onset of senescence. For example, in the "Debat du jeune et du vieulx amoureux," a lover suddenly becomes old and retires from the court of love; to a young man just entering the court he explains this change with the basic truism of medieval dichotomized senescence—"After youth, whoever does not die becomes old."[38] The fading of the flower of youth is often dramatized as an abrupt attack:

> Little by little the years accumulate,
> And we are oblivious to this;
> Then, suddenly, old age unexpectedly
> Comes upon the mortal body in various ways,
> And upon its back puts the icicles
> Of infirmity, weakness, and pain,
> Until in the end death leads it away.[39]

Usually associated with these icicles of infirmity, weakness, and pain is a series of psychological and moral changes. Often associated with aging are avarice, envy, jealousy, and hypocrisy, vices portrayed with Vielleice on the wall outside the garden of amorous delight, vices which render the senescent even less capable of love.

On the whole, medieval descriptions of older people and representations of a personified Age—a distinction that is usually only nominal—form a dismal, pathetic image of the years after 30 or 40. Virtually all such works exclude sexual activity in *senectus*. Yet the mythic contrast of Youth and Age is so sharply polarized that there is little written about the momentous change itself, the actual passage from the realm of Venus to the realm of Saturn. Perhaps the most developed representation of sexual senescence—the conversion from courtly values to Christian, from physical love to divine, from folly to reason, from worldly joy to repentance and *contemptus mundi,* from life to death—is to be found in the *Confessio Amantis.*

Sexual Senescence in the "Confessio Amantis"

This work begins with the topos of May, a lover, and a dream, as does *Le Roman de la Rose;* but here the Lover is frustrated in his pursuit of love. Venus orders him to confess before considering his request for a cure for his affliction. Her priest Genius then reviews in fine encyclopedic fashion the Seven Deadly Sins, with an emphasis on lovers, for over 30,000 lines. The Lover finds himself guilty of only a few minor sins; his pursuit of love has been quite virtuous. Genius advises him, nonetheless, to abandon thoughts of earthly love, but he is unable to dissuade the Lover, who insists that Venus either withdraw the burning dart of love or grant him the "salve" that he desires. Venus quickly succeeds where her priest has failed. She points out the nature of the Lover's sin—his age—and refuses to allow him the satisfaction of his love. Soon after, the cure is made complete: Cupid removes his dart, and with cold salve, not the warm "salve" of love requited, Venus anoints his head, heart, and loins.[40]

We find in the *Confessio Amantis* the mythology of sexual senescence as developed by the confluence of Christianity and courtly love. When the goddess of love refuses to consider the plea of the would-be Lover until he has confessed to her priest, she turns the Lover over to the voice of moral and social responsibility. When the priest is unable to persuade the Lover to accept that law which is governed by reason and not by desire, Venus resorts to shock treatment. She is not interested in his feelings of love, no matter how courtly or virtuous. In pointing out the physiology of *senectus,* she destroys the spirit of *juventus*.

The dampening effect of Venus' bluntness is only temporary, however. The feelings of the Lover are so strong that he renounces earthly love only after Cupid removes the dart of passion. This supernatural intervention is necessary because his natural instincts are still vigorous, despite his age; certain members of the jury of lovers express the judgment, underscored by a marginal "Nota," that

> The wild madness of love
> In man's life does not yield to Age;
> As long as there is oil to set afire,
> The lamp is easily lit,
> And it is very difficult to extinguish it,
> Except if it is in a saint,
> Preserved by the grace of God.[41]

To put the finishing touch on the cure, Venus then shows the Lover his appearance in a "wonder Mirour." We are to understand this mirror, it seems, as a symbol of objective self-assessment:

Wherein I cast my heart's eye
At once, and saw my pale complexion,
My eyes dull and devoid of joy,
My thin cheeks; and I saw
My face disfigured with Age,
So wrinkled and so woeful in appearance,
That there was nothing full or smooth.
I also saw my hoary hair.
Then I no longer felt any desire to see
My appearance, for there was no pleasure in it.[42]

Resignation to physiological decline is possible only after the extinction of sexual desire. The Lover attains sainthood when he abandons physical love for spiritual, crossing the great divide from courtly interests to Christian.

At what age is Venus setting this mandatory retirement from amorous activity? Gower gives us no precise indication of the Lover's age. If we consider the *Confessio Amantis* autobiographical in this detail, which may not be so, we might assign the Lover the age at which Gower wrote this work, perhaps 60 to 70.[43] His reference to May and December is proverbial, and it would suggest an age in the middle to late fifties. Yet, when the Lover compares the course of life to the months of the year, he mentions only that he has passed September, which implies that he may be just in his middle forties.[44] Probably the influence of the rhetorical tradition makes his description seem more appropriate to a later age.

Senectus

Old age as a time of reason and wisdom, of freedom from passions, the rule of mind and soul over body, such as we find it praised by Plato, Cicero, and Seneca, has little place in medieval European literature.[45] Between the courtly values of youth and worldly delights and the Christian values of *contemptus mundi* and the afterlife, old age is both an end and a beginning, but little else, a time of regrets and preparation, but not enjoyment. In "The Prais of Aige" (late 15th C.)

Henryson has "ane ald man and decrepit" sing of being glad to be old; yet his praise of aging is actually praise of death as deliverance from the vanity of life, as summarized in his refrain, "The older we become, the closer to heavenly bliss."[46] This is a common moral theme: old age is good because long experience leads to a better understanding of the emptiness of worldly things, the mutability of fortune, and the dangers of the passions. In this view, old age is judged to be not a stage of life but the threshold of death.

Even when the medieval writers claim that senescence has the advantage of freedom from passions, they point out that this freedom never is assured. At any time the madness of love may endanger whatever contentment and wisdom can be found in later years. Perhaps the best known example occurs in "Le Lay d'Aristote" told by Henri d'Andeli (early 12th century) and many others. Sexual desire leads the wise old philosopher to play the horse for a young, beautiful woman. The great anguish with which he later recognizes his folly dramatizes the moral lesson of his story:

> Oh, no! Where are my senses?
>
> . . . .
>
> Even I, who am filled with old age,
> Cannot do battle against Love.[47]

Medieval European literature offers abundant examples of the problems resulting when older people become sexually involved with younger people—fabliaux, 'malmariée' poems, the lays "Guigemar" and "Yonec," "The Miller's Tale," and the story of Lidia and Nicostrato in the *Decameron*, to mention only a few dramatizations of the belief that age and youth cannot live together. Philippe de Novare warns especially against pairing an older man with a younger woman, a situation in which the man risks being robbed of his possessions and/or living in constant fear of being cuckolded. Deschamps claims that an old man cannot hasten his death more than by marrying a woman of fifteen, and that such a man will die miserable within three years. This refrain echoes the old German proverb,

> A young woman married to an old man
> Provides him with a horse that will carry him to his grave.

This same thought is expressed more acrimoniously in the *Arcipreste de Talavera* (1438): "For the young man a beautiful young woman, and may the rancid old woman be burned; and for the young woman a charming young man, and may the boring old man burst."[48]

It is not only misalliance that brings reproach upon older people, however; any manner of sexual involvement is criticized. Philippe de Novare warns against the marriage of two old people, that is, over 60, because "two things rotting in one bed is not at all proper."[49] We find the same sentiment expressed in the *Lamentations de Mahieu* (ca. 1370), with the suggestion of community disapproval:

> And if an old man takes an old woman
> It is not surprising if he is reproved for this;
> For it is contrary to what is right and what is customary
> In old age and in marriage.[50]

Alfonso Martinez de Toledo states in the *Arcipreste de Talavera:* "There is still another kind of marriage to be condemned (. . .), that is, when an old man marries an old woman, for there will never be anything but scolding and quarreling on both sides."[51]

In this respect at least, Philippe de Novare seems representative of the mainstream of medieval European thought. Of the three worst sinners mentioned in Ecclesiastes 25:2 he puts in first place the "dirty old man," shameful to God and to the world: "If he lusts after any woman whatsoever, that is a very vile sin and an outrage, this desire without purpose; for even though the desire is there, the power is completely gone."[52] Yet it is not lack of ability to perform sexual acts that makes this interest in sex a sin and an outrage, for he also chastises women, although they do not lose their ability, but only their youth and beauty.[53] Medieval writers create a number of examples, all negative, of older women involved in sexual matters, among which Richeut and Hersent, the Vetula, the Vieille Truande, and the Corbaccio, this last a woman only in her middle forties.[54] Quite simply, upon passing into *senectus* a person is expected to abandon sexual interests, "to look and act his or her age."[55]

In *The Praise of Folly* (1509), the great humanist Erasmus

has Folly describe the behavior of older people who still enjoy the pleasures of life: "The less reason they have for remaining alive, the more they seem to delight in living (. . .). You see them still enjoying life so much and trying to be young so hard (. . .). These capers are laughed at by everyone, with good reason, as being the silliest in the world."[56] In this passage we find several concepts basic to the medieval mythology of senescence: *senectus* is the threshold of death, the pleasures of love and of life in general are only for *juventus,* and those who fail to respect this 'natural order' are guilty of extreme folly.

In considering literary characters who continue their sexual activity beyond *juventus,* mention must be made of others who without trying to remain lovers also refuse to leave the realm of Venus. They assume the functions of guardians, intermediaries, or teachers. The old woman in *The Romance of the Rose* is an excellent example of all three roles: she guards the Rose against love, she arranges with the Lover to facilitate his advances, and she teaches the Rose how best to profit from the game of love. These functions have been the subject of numerous studies;[57] in brief, older people engaging in such ancillary activities are treated with very little sympathy in medieval European literature. Although occasionally an older intermediary may be depicted as serving the interests of both parties with the best of intentions, in general these guardians, intermediaries, and teachers are considered subversive to society and/or enemies of love, *senectus* out of place in the world of *juventus.*

Conclusion

In summary, medieval authors seem little interested in aging as a gradual and individual process. Although a long line of works present various schemes for the division of life into stages, the tendency in literature is to polarize, to reduce these divisions to the most basic, the dichotomy of *juventus* and *senectus,* associating a wide range of physiological, psychological, and moral traits with either one or the other of these idealized states. The senescent person, around age 30 in women and age 40 in men, passes between the two very different worlds of *juventus* and *senectus* which seem to have no real point of contact. The Christian ethic exhorts the senescent person to withdraw from the rest of society, to turn his or her thoughts and energies toward death and salvation. The courtly ethic also promotes this separation, finding elders' presence to be detrimental to the amorous activities of the young. As the aged figure constitutes an allegorical *memento mori* (remember that you shall die), the senescent—who may be only 30 or 40—constitutes a *memento senescere* (remember that you are growing old).

Whether this moral is expressed or merely implied, the use of the *juventus-senectus* dichotomy serves as a sobering reminder to young lovers of the impending necessity of passing from erotic pleasures to material cares, social responsibilities, and contempt for the vanity of the world, from an amorous and amoral microcosm to the surrounding realm of morality. Sexual senescence represents the necessity, natural to some extent, of course, but particularly social and moral, of abandoning the pursuit of the Rose, of turning from life toward death, of leaving the Lover in order to become the pathetic portrait of old age in exile outside the Garden of Love, a relatively short and insignificant step from death.

We end as we began, at the wall described in *The Romance of the Rose.* With the portrait of old age, Guillaume de Lorris gives us also a fairly long description of the nature of Time, which suggests that Vielleice represents *senectus,* not only the final years of life. Although he describes Time as a constant flow, a natural part of this description is the division of life into two stages, the period of time "in which all things are nourished and grow" and the period of time "in which all things wear out and rot." In these lines we recognize with the medieval public the conventional dichotomy of *juventus* and *senectus,* with all of their established associations—the time of the Rose and the time of old age, separated by the high wall of sexual senescence.

2

CELESTINA: THE AGING PROSTITUTE AS WITCH

By Javier Herrero

[We have already seen the reviling of the old, and especially of old women, in medieval literature. Perhaps surprisingly, misogyny and ageism acquired particular *virulence during the early Renaissance, when old women were persecuted as witches. The uses of magic had created intrigue and sometimes even fun in medieval fiction (for example in the often playful "matière de Bretagne," based on Celtic myths). But by the time of Fernando de Rojas' writing of* La Celestina *(around 1500), the elements of the fantastic had taken on a more sinister cast, being associated with heresy. Rojas, a converted Jew, wrote in an atmosphere of vigilantism in which Jews were persecuted as heretics by Papal decree. Living at a time when conversion was no longer sufficient to deter the cruelty of Christian persecutions,[1] Rojas, as a* converso, *may have sought a substitute to put under the spotlight, the archetypal old woman-prostitute-witch. Like the stereotypical Jewish moneylender, she is cunning and avaricious. But she is also willfully evil.*

Before the period in which Rojas was writing, the insane, deranged and senile enjoyed a brief respite from the most severe condemnations, during which a distinction was made between "voluntary possession, in which a person deliberately made a pact with the devil, and involuntary possession, in which the unfortunate individual, against his will, was simply invaded by the devil."[2] *By the time of Rojas' writing the Church had become more severe again, and all deranged persons were considered to be witches and sorcerers. A few decades later, the great witch hunts began, and thousands upon thousands were tortured, drowned, or burned. By far the most numerous victims were old women.*

Not that the fictional character, Celestina, *is deranged. The aging prostitute who is the main character in the tragicomedy of the same name is a witch of the voluntary sort. As Professor Herrero shows so well, Celestina uses youth for vicarious sexual fulfillment. By encouraging the young to profit from current corruptions, she perverts the role of the wise old person who remembers a golden age of moral superiority. Celestina makes no scruple of depicting age as advantageous, or as a terrible burden, according to the necessities of the situation. Although she is evidently the most energetic and fit of all the characters, she sometimes uses the supposed ills of old age as an excuse: "I've been too ill and worried to visit you as I should, but God knows my good intentions"; "old age is nothing but an inn of infirmities." Because she contradicts herself, we don't know what to believe. We have little or no idea of how she actually experiences old age. In a sense, this sets her outside of the experience of human aging, reinforcing her image as a supernatural being—Eds.]*

CELESTINA is one of the most powerful old women in world literature, sly, articulate, skillful and evil. Prostitute and witch, she casts a web in which all the characters of the *tragicomedia* are caught and devoured,[1] and finally falls victim to her own grim craft. Let us briefly outline the plot: Calisto, an elegant young gentleman, follows his falcon to the orchard of Melibea; upon seeing her, he is possessed by a mad passion which allows him to think of nothing else; his servant, Sempronio, advises him to use the help of the old bawd and shrewd go-between called Celestina; a good servant, Pármeno, warns him against it, but is soon corrupted by Celestina; the old woman entices Calisto into making her extravagant gifts; Celestina conjures the devil and with the help of a potion, in which she soaks a skein of wool, bewitches Melibea, who yields to Calisto's entreaties; Sempronio and Pármeno claim their part of the bounty; Celestina's greed makes her miscalculate: she thinks that she can talk them out of their anger at being short-changed, but they kill her and in turn are executed; Calisto attends an assignation with Melibea at night in her orchard, while his servants keep watch; he hears noises. Thinking that his guards might need help, he climbs the wall in haste, falls to the ground and is killed; Melibea commits suicide; and the work ends with her father's powerful and desperate plaint.

A World of Witchcraft

The world of *La Celestina* is dominated by the devil, who brings the characters to destruction through lust and greed.[2] Lust hovers as a dark cloud over the book, and its lightning inflames and burns its victims. This world should be understood as a conflict of two great powers: God, embodied in His Church, the Body of Christ; and the devil, who, through the counter-church of the witches' covens, tries to overthrow the Lord's Kingdom.[3] In the late Middle Ages and early Renaissance there seemed to be a general agreement that although devils can cause evil directly, they usually act through the intermediary of witches. There are several reasons for this. Since man's soul is free, the devil can drag him to sin only by affecting his senses and feelings, which finally move the will with irresistible force.[4] This chaining of the will is best achieved through exciting man's sensuality:

> Although they have a thousand ways of doing harm, . . . yet their power remains confined to the privy parts and the navel. . . . For through the wantonness of the flesh they have much power over men; and in men the source of wantonness lies in the privy parts, since it is from them that the semen falls, just as in women it falls from the navel (p. 24).

But devils, being spirits, need the instrumental help of witches to affect human sensuality and to inflict their destruction on men's souls and on Nature; witchcraft, then, is a child of evil and lust: "All witchcraft comes from carnal lust, which is in women insatiable".[5] The coupling of devil and witch takes place through a pact, of which the most solemn moment is the oath: "(T)he devil demands the following oath of homage to himself: that she gives herself to him, body and soul, forever, and does her utmost to bring others of both sexes into his power" (p. 100).[6] By this pact the devil claims for himself the adoration due to God: "It is obvious that his principal motive is to offer the greater offense to the Divine Majesty by usurping to himself a creature dedicated to God" (p. 10). We see then, that the pact is the beginning of a frantic task of proselytizing, of which the witch is the principal agent, and whose aim is a profound subversion of values by which the devil will finally replace God in the heart of men. The Serpent corrupted love through lust and in this way caused the first couple to sin and fall. Witches continue the task which the devil started in Paradise. The higher the victim, the more effective will be the havoc caused by his or her downfall. Through the depravation of morals, the devil and witches hope to fulfill the task of the serpent.

How terrible this depravity was believed to be at the end of the 15th century is made obvious by the dreadful bull *Summis desiderantes affectibus* of 9 December, 1484, which Innocent VIII addressed to Henry Kramer and James Sprenger, authors of the *Malleus Maleficarum*. Although bulls against witchcraft were not unusual during the 13th and 14th centuries, and in the 15th practically no Pope had reigned without issuing one or several, what makes *Summis desiderantes affectibus* significant is the sense of panic it conveys, and the encouragement given to the authors of the *Malleus,* Sprenger and Kramer, as Inquisitors, to unleash a persecution which was to light fires all over central Europe, burning thousands of unfortunate creatures, mostly old women: "They showed themselves most zealous in the work which they had to do, and especially did they make inquisition for witches and for those who were gravely suspect of sorcery, all of whom they prosecuted with the extremest rigour of the law."[7] The *Malleus,* then, directing the work of the Inquisitors whom the Pope had charged with the destruction of witchcraft, provided the program of the repression, and enjoyed immense popularity at the end of the 15th and during the 16th and 17th centuries.[8] The *Malleus,* the bull itself, and, of course, the fact of the persecutions, gave a frightening relevance to witchcraft in the years in which *La Celestina* was conceived and written.

Celestina: "Puta vieja alcoholada" ("drunken old whore") and diabolic seamstress.

When Celestina is first described in the book by Sempronio, the corrupt servant of Calisto, she is defined with features which bring her very close to the descriptions of witches given in the *Malleus*. She can incite lust even in the coldest:

> It is now a good while ago, since at the lower end of this street I fell acquainted with an old bearded woman called Celestina, a witch[9], subtle as the devil, and well-practiced in all the evils that the world can afford, I mean one who has married and restored a hundred thousand maidenheads in this city: such a power and such authority she hath, by her persuasions and other cunning devices, that none escape her; she will move the very stones to lust if she chooses.[10]

This grim picture is confirmed and expanded by the good and faithful servant Pármeno, who warns Calisto against the evil deeds of the old woman and the dangers of employing her services for the seduction of Melibea. Pármeno knew her well; in fact, as an innocent child, he had been her servant and had lived at her house. When Sempronio first brings Celestina to Calisto's house to discuss her employment as a go-between, Pármeno refers to her as a "puta vieja alcoholada" (Act I; p. 251). Her profession, Pármeno continues, is that of seamstress or embroiderer,[11] but under it she covers the less honorable one of "a perfumeress, a former of faces, a mender of cracked maidenheads, a bawd and had something of a witch about her." Her sewing is not only a cover for her pernicious activities, but also an ironic metaphor for them. With the pretext of her sewing and embroidery, "many young wenches that were of your ordinary sorts of servants, came to the house to work, some on smocks, some on gorgets and many other things." They all brought victuals to her, which had been stolen from their houses, ". . . and other thefts of higher caliber, making her house (for she was the receiver, and kept all things close) the rendezvous of all their roguery." But this first corruption was only one step toward their initiation into servitude to lust and whoredom: "She was a great friend to students, noblemen's caterers, and pages: to these she sold the innocent blood of these poor miserable souls who risked their virginity, drawn on by fair promises and the restitution and reparation which she would make of their lost maidenheads" (Act I, pp. 26–27).

Through servants, then, Celestina proceeds to the corruption of "las más encerradas" ("*those most carefully guarded*"): "And these, in especially religious days, such as *via crucis,* processions by night, midnight masses, masses at dawn and other secret devotions, many of these, covered with veils, I saw going into her house."[12] This mixture of the sacred with the obscene transforms religious references into blasphemies, a sign of diabolical activity. The days chosen by the devil to copulate with witches are "the most sacred times of the whole year, such as Christmas, Easter, Pentecost, and other Feast Days": the reason is "that in this way witches may become imbued not only with the vice of perfidy through apostasy from the Faith, but also with that of sacrilege, and that greater offense may be done to the Creator" (*Malleus,* 113). Of course, Celestina's victims are not witches; but it is she who chooses the days and places of their assignations. By replacing a devotional activity with a lustful one, a deeper corruption is implanted into the sins of her women. Such corruption, in the universally accepted beliefs of the time, could have its source only in diabolical inspiration. Celestina does not spare the Church itself; she makes of the holy retreat of friars and nuns her market place: "Yet notwithstanding all these cares she never missed the mass or the vespers, and spent her time in monasteries of friars and nuns; they were the markets where she made her bargains."[13] It was, above all, in the stitching of the hymen that her work as an embroiderer excelled:

> For the mending of lost maidenheads, she used bladders, or stitched them up with a needle. She had in a little painted work-box certain fine small needles, such as your glovers sow with, and threads of the slenderest and smallest silk, ruffed over with wax: she had also roots hanging there of folia-plasm, fuste-sanguino, squill or sea-onion, and ground thistle. With these she did work wonders; and

> when the French ambassador came there, she sold one of her girls three times for a virgin (Act I, p. 29).

The needle becomes, in Celestina's hand, a form of diabolic sacrament: it erases the wages of sin and restores the recipient to a state of desirability which prepares her anew for lustful initiations.

The Timeless Will

Celestina is quite aware of the ravages of time, of the immense diminution which the loss of youth and beauty, even of the charms of middle age, imply for a prostitute whose livelihood depends upon her attractiveness, her ability to be well received, and to penetrate into the hearts and abodes of others—especially the rich and powerful. Her looks, charm, and energy allowed her, in the plenitude of her powers, to reign over an empire of vice; in her old age, however, the wheel of her Fortune is sinking: "[M]y honor did mount to that height, as was fitting for a woman of my quality to rise unto; and now of force, it must descend and fall as much. By this I know that I am near my end, and that the lease of my life is now expiring" (Act IX, p. 150). The zenith of her "honor" consisted in possessing "nine gallant young wenches . . . the eldest was not above eighteen, and not one of them under fourteen". Through them Celestina gained a prestigious clientele: "Old gentlemen, young ones, abbots of all ranks, from bishops to sextons". She penetrated the ramparts of the Church and brought the worship of the flesh to the heart of Christ's servants:

> In entering a Church, as many hats went off to me as if I were a duchess: he who had the least business with me considered himself the lowest. When they spied me half a league off, they would forsake the Choir, one by one, two by two, and come to me, to see if I wanted anything, each asking about his lover. . . . One would call me mistress, another aunt, others their love, others honest old woman. There they would decide when they should come to my house, there they would agree when I should go to theirs, there they would offer me money, there they would make me promises, there likewise present me with gifts: some kissing my coat, and some my cheek, to please me better.[14]

Such is her authority that she commands the most abject servitude in the house of God itself: she has, in fact, transformed it into a brothel! However, we begin to see in her speech the pride which will cause her downfall: she does not fully realize that she is, above all, an agent; that this hommage is rendered through her to the prince of lust, from whom her own power obtains. Her strength comes from her lord; and her lord is a dangerous ally.

Celestina's skill, of course, is immense. In her first meeting with Melibea, Celestina draws a grim picture of the evils of old age in order to convince the girl to enjoy her youth:

> [old age] is nothing else but a very spittle-house of diseases, an inn full of infirmities, a storehouse of sad and melancholy thoughts, a friend to wrangling and brawling, a continual grief and incurable plague; pitying that which is past, punished in that which is present, and full of wretched worry for what's to come; a near neighbor of death; a poor cabin without one bough of shelter, into which it rains from all sides; a willow wand, a staff of weak osier, which is bent double with the least stress you put it to.

This picture reflects Celestina's experience of the weakness which has deprived her of her empire; but let us not forget that in this dialogue the old woman is darkening her own image to make Melibea especially aware of the charms of her own youth, and to move her to enjoy her senses while they are in full bloom: "God grant she [Melibea] may long enjoy her noble youth and this her flourishing prime, a time wherein most pleasures and delights are found" (Act IV; p. 69). The theme of "old age versus youth" is used by the shrewd old woman to elicit sympathy and to talk the young into illicit sex. A world of handsome young men and pretty girls, engaged in a passionate libertinage, unconcerned with fears or regrets; that is the picture that she gives to the youths of the *tragicomedia,* not only to seduce them, but also to vicariously enjoy her own lust. When Celestina is set on seducing Pármeno into being an accomplice in the exploitation of Calisto's passion, she opens her attack by referring directly to the boy's sexual organ: "You must have a hard time keeping the point of your belly down!"[15] This frankness, which provokes Pármeno's laughter, opens the way to Celestina's attack on the boy's loyalty to his lord through his chastity. Urged to imitate Sempronio, Pármeno answers: "I have heard old men say that one example of lechery or greed does much harm, and that a man should deal only with those who may make him better." Celestina scolds him for his restraint, and displays a joyful picture of youths in blossom devoted to the search of pleasure:

> You're talking nonsense, for without company there is no pleasure in the possession of anything. Don't draw back then, don't torment and vex thyself. For Nature shuns whatsoever savors of sadness, and desires that which is pleasant and delightful. And delight is with friends, in things that are sensual; but especially in recounting matters of love, and communicating them, the one to the other. . . . O what speech! what grace! what sport! what kisses! (Act I; p. 41).

Pármeno recognizes the corruption and heresy in these maxims. He says that she preaches as those who "have invited and drawn men to drink of their heresies, sugaring their cup with some sweet kind of poison."[16] Such an accusation, in the late 15th century, and spoken by a boy who has just described Celestina to Calisto as an old witch, can only be an accusation of witchcraft. But the poison already absorbed by Pármeno is too strong and sweet, and after awakening the young man's lust, Celestina ends her work of corruption by bringing him to Areusa, who will teach him the way of the flesh, the door to brief joy followed by his and Celestina's death.

Intelligence, experience, and courage endow old age with almost irresistible power in Celestina. The weakness she claims is like the dry and withered branches which cover a deadly trap; it hides, in its dark recess, the poisoned blades of a corrupted but sharp intelligence and a firm will, strengthened by the devil's favor. Part of this game of apparent weakness is her claim to be seen as a kindly old adviser, an infirm but loving mother. To her the young may come in search of good advice:

> But you young men care not for us that are old, but live only for your own pleasure. You never think about sickness; it never occurs to you that the flower of your youth will wither. But mark my words, friend: in such cases of necessity as these, an old woman (be she well-experienced)

> is a good help, a comforter, a friend, a mother, nay, more than a mother; a good inn to give rest when you're well, and a good hospital when you're ill (Act VII; p. 109).

Yet this "comforter", this "mother, nay, more than a mother", gives deadly advice, by subverting language in the most astonishing way. In order to persuade Pármeno to betray his master, Celestina uses Seneca's maxims in praise of true friendship: "For, as Seneca saith, 'Travellers have many inns and few friends' . . . Therefore, my good son, leave off these violences of youth, and following the doctrine and rule of thy ancestors, return to reason, settle thyself in some one place or other." So far, it is pure Senecan advice: get for your soul a permanent abode, which is the good, and consider the world's attachment as temporary. But this is certainly not Celestina's interpretation; rather, it means that Pármeno should continue to serve Calisto as long as it is profitable. Such service, however, must be without the "foolish loyalty and ignorant honesty" which Pármeno had given to his master so far: instead, such loyalty would be given to his true friends, Sempronio and Celestina, and the aim of this new friendship would be, through their joint efforts, to rob his master Calisto.

Modern research has shown the great amount of classical and especially Stoic learning which is skillfully woven into Celestina's exuberant prose. The whole tradition of classical rhetoric is subverted in the service of sensuality. Her speech is also, of course, overlaid with the popular wisdom of idioms and proverbs. With uncanny sharpness Celestina submits the morals embodied in these proverbs to the same distortion which we have seen applied to Seneca's maxim, in her attempt to persuade Elicia's cousin Areusa (a young prostitute who feels she owes fidelity to her absent lover) to give herself to Pármeno.

Celestina also supports her advice with a barrage of popular wisdom which acquires an obscene meaning in her mouth: "The meanest creature on earth is the mouse that hath but one hole to trust to; for if it's stopped, she hath no means to hide herself from the cat . . . " (Act VII; p. 122) Celestina spits out a whole string of legal, natural, and moral maxims and proverbs, each based on the theme that two are better than one, cunningly mixed and twisted to make a legitimate-sounding argument.

Celestina succeeds; Pármeno breaks the bonds of loyalty to his master and Areusa to her lover as Pármeno discovers the joys of the flesh in Areusa's arms and becomes a faithful instrument in the hands of Celestina. Victory over the forces of good is only one aim of the brilliant strategist; the old woman needs youth in order vicariously to satisfy her own lust. The encounter of Areusa and Pármeno provides an example of Celestina's partially successful search for pleasure. When Celestina arrives with Pármeno to Areusa' house, having boldly promised the young man that she will deliver the girl to him, she asks Pármeno to wait at the foot of the stairs and quickly walks up to Areusa's room. The girl has just undressed to go to bed. Celestina approaches the bed and with delight uncovers her body and touches her: "O how like a siren you look! How fair, how beautiful! O how sweet everything smells about you, when you turn in your bed." But sight and smell are not enough for Celestina: "[M]y pearl, my jewel of gold, see whether I love you or not, that I come to visit you at this time of night! Let my eye take its fill in beholding you; it does me much good to touch you, and to look upon you" (Act VII; pp. 111–118). Areusa explains to Celestina that she is going early to bed because she feels ill. This, of course, gives Celestina a new excuse to continue with her caresses:

> Celestina: Go to, give me leave a little to touch you; and I will try what I can do . . .
>
> Areusa: Lay your hand higher up towards my stomach.
>
> Celestina: God bless you and Saint Michael Archangel! How plump and fresh you are! What lovely breasts! I thought you beautiful, when I saw what everybody could see, but now I tell you that, as far as I can judge, there are not three bodies in town as beautiful as yours (Act VII; p. 118).[17]

Finally, Celestina persuades Areusa to receive Pármeno in her bed and invites him to make love to her while she watches: "Come here you, lazy timid one; I want to see how much you are worth before I go; enjoy here in this bed!" When Areusa begs that he should wait until Celestina is gone, the old woman feigns to be outraged: "What is this, Areusa? What is this puzzlement, and shyness, this novelty and shamefulness? Do you think that I don't know what this is? That I have not seen a man and a woman together?" Areusa repents and submits: "Mother, please, if I erred, I beg you pardon. Come as close as you want, and let him do whatever he pleases!"[18] The coldness of Celestina's old age is warmed by the vicarious enjoyment of youth's lust; if Celestina preys on the beauty and wealth of her patrons, it is not only for greed's sake. She frankly acknowledges the losses of age, but can partially recover her lost youth as she hovers pruriently over the joys of her prey. When she finally leaves the couple, it is because she has become sexually frustrated: "Good-bye now! I can't stand your kissing and romping. The taste of it's still in my mouth—I didn't lose it with my teeth!"

One cannot deny the withering of the body, one cannot recover the freshness of youth, by will alone. Only a state of sustained illusion can bring us back (albeit only temporarily) to paradise. In a grotesque dinner, which seems to be a sacrilegious parody of the Last Supper, Celestina sings the praises of wine which gives her not eternal life, but the illusion of eternal youth. Elicia and Areusa sit by their lovers, Sempronio and Pármeno; Celestina sits, she says, by her own lover: a jug of wine:

> Sit down, my children, there's room for everybody, thank God; I hope we can get as much room in Heaven when we go there. Let everyone take his place, as he likes, and sit next to his love: I, who am alone, will sit down here by this jug of wine . . . Ever since I started getting old, I know no better office at table than to pour wine . . . With this I line all my clothes at Christmas: this warms my blood, keeps me in one piece, makes me merry, where'er I go; this makes me look fresh and ruddy as a rose . . . This drives away all care and sorrow from the heart better than gold and coral; this gives strength to the young man, and vigor to the old . . . " (Act IX; pp. 140–141).[19]

Warmed by the wine and living sensually through the flesh of the young couples, she encourages them to crown the enjoyment of the meal with that of the body: "Go to, enjoy yourselves while you may . . . Fall to your flap, kiss and clip; here, at the table, everything from the waist up is permissible . . . How nice it is to see you play, you little devils! . . . Watch! Don't upset the table!" (Act IX, p. 146).[20]

Presiding over this grim banquet and praising the glories of wine, restorer of freshness, comforter, dispenser of strength and joy; the image of sensual plenitude before her, and that she encourages, revives the memory of her own youth and of past glories. The memory of her loss saddens her and she begins to reminisce. But Areusa says, "For God's sake, we came here to have a good time", and Sempronio cruelly pierces her dream as later he will stab her body: "There's no use crying over the good old days if you can't get them back . . . You're spoiling our good time, so clear the table" (Act IX: p. 153). Even the wily witch is limited in her magic.

The Part of the Devil: "Philocaptio"

We have, so far, seen Celestina cast a vast net in which she entangles her victims. We shall examine now, how, with the help of the devil, she exercises her craft. Peter Russell went, in my opinion, to the heart of *La Celestina* when he stated: "[T]he main thematic function of La Celestina in the work of Rojas is to produce, by the means of a pact with the Devil, a case of *philocaptio* whose victim is Melibea".[21] *Philocaptio* is "inordinate love of one person for another" and can be caused either by the concupiscence of human nature, or by direct intervention of the devil, or, finally, by the spells of witches with the help of the devils.[22] In the last case, witches can "so inflame their hearts that by no shame or punishment, by no words or actions can they be forced to desist from such love."[23] To this third case, of course, belongs the passion inflamed in the heart of Melibea by Celestina.

The bewitchment of Melibea is the center of a complex net of relationships which extend to the whole *tragicomedia* and serve as a unifying structure through which the most frightening elements of witchcraft are represented; by means of these elements the presence of the devil, and his hold over the characters, is expressed. As we shall show in the following pages, the rites, instruments, and spells which Celestina uses to cause the *philocaptio* of Melibea were the commonplace means of contemporary witchcraft, and would be easily recognized as such by late 15th-century readers; such instruments are the signs of an obscene world of lust and greed which, once understood, sheds a sinister light on the work and conveys to us with vivid clarity its irresistible power. In a chapter entitled "Spells, filters, fumigations and amatory charms," Sebastián Cirac Estopañán writes of the world of superstitions which surfaces through Celestina's spells: "Alive and energetic beats the pagan spirit in the pages which we read here. They reveal to us ideas and feelings in which the most beastly vice is expressed, a vice, which corrupts the soul and quenches the light of the spirit. Here we shall meet a furious lust, with all its exaltation and all its abominations . . . and lust itself will introduce to us its priestesses, the Castillian Celestinas, diligent and shrewd."[24] We shall briefly describe Celestina's incantation and then carefully examine its elements.

In Act III, speaking with Sempronio, Celestina says: "I always carry a little parcel of yarn and other trinkets as bait, that I may have some pretext to make my easier entrance and access, where they don't know me . . . " (Act III; p. 59) This yarn will be the "bait" and, as we shall see, the instrument of the devil's *philocaptio*. The yarn is, in fact, the means by which the devil is literally introduced in Melibea's house.[25] To produce her charm Celestina uses a paper written with bat's blood, blood and hair of a goat, and serpent's oil. The bat and the goat are signs of the devil, and the serpent's oil is a major element in the structure of the *tragicomedia*. Its symbolic power embraces and pervades all the other instruments and metaphors. The aim of the charm is to make the devil present in the yarn through the agency of the serpent's oil with which she anoints it, and to entangle Melibea in the yarn until she becomes subservient to the will of Celestina. With this entanglement, the masterful spider captures high and lowly in a web of lust which threatens the moral fabric of the community.

Death of the Old Spider

Melibea is only one among the many victims of Celestina's

craft. In her we have had a chance to study in detail the brilliant strategy of the old bawd and, through it, the ruthlessness and strength of her spirit. Celestina approaches every possible victim with the same cold cruelty: she prepares her net and watches from afar. Early in the third act Sempronio expresses his awe of Celestina's experience: "This is not the first business thou hast taken in hand." Celestina replies:

> The first, my son? Few virgins (praise the Lord) have you seen open shop in this town, whose wares I've not been the first to peddle. When a baby girl is born, I write her down in my register, and keep a catalogue of all their names, so that I might know how many escaped my net (Act III, p. 55).

The yarn used to entangle Melibea is, then, only a fragment of the vast thread employed to build a net as great as the city itself. This is the real employment of her profession of seamstress. And how profitably Celestina has used it we saw earlier: in her golden years, when her body was still in bloom and could faithfully serve her sharp mind and her passions, she built an empire which dared to break through the ramparts of the Church and claim obedience in the temple itself. But Celestina, who outwits the wittier opponents, does not seem to be able to outwit mortality; not even her accomplice, the devil, will help her in this. Lust and greed are not the only passions which rage in Celestina's soul. Greed, as we know, is the direct cause of her death. But a sinful pride enters too.

She rejoices in victory: to tame and to break a young maid, a virgin who rebels against her, provides her with a joy of Sadean intensity. She describes the taming of Melibea on several occasions and in each one she debases the young girl by comparing her to animals. Melibea, she boasts to Calisto, is like a hen who has not yet been subdued by the cock: "For though Melibea be brave, she's not the first one whom with God's blessing I have made to stoop and leave her cackling"; she is like a wild mare which must be broken to the saddle: "they are all given to bucking and rearing; but after they once suffer the saddle on their backs, they never want to rest. They should like to ride forever; sooner dead than tired." Especially so those who, like Melibea, hide their fire under outer coldness:

"[T]hey entreat him, of whom they were entreated; they endure torment for him, by whom they were tormented; they are servants to those who once served them" (Act III; p. 58).[26] In Act VI Celestina describes to Calisto the surrender of Melibea: her fall is compared to the striking of a bull by the matador, and Celestina takes a matador's pride in her accomplishments as aggressor. Moreover, the miscalculation which brings about her own assassination is due to hubris: she who had talked so many girls into her net, thought that Sempronio and Pármeno could be talked out of their share of the profits gained by the ruin of Melibea. But she is mistaken. When they find Celestina unmoved by prayers, entreaties, and threats, Sempronio cries: "Miserly old woman, dying of thirst for money!" (Act XII; pp. 192–193). Indeed she is; Celestina still refuses, and Sempronio, encouraged by Pármeno, stabs the old bawd, who dies asking vainly for absolution: "Ay me, I am slain. Ay, ay! Confession, confession!" (Act XII; p. 193). None is to be had, for the "honor" that she sought through the perfection of her crimes was not legitimate self-approval, but sinful pride.

A Possessed World

We can see now with some clarity several features of Celestina's complex soul. Like the Sadean hero she is utterly alone; her relationship with the other is one of agent to instrument. Through it she searches for profit, pleasure, honor. But these features are the expression of one more profound: the exaltation of the Self in the possession of the other, in the reduction of the adversary to victim. This erotic hunt, however, implies some stark contradictions which finally destroy Celestina.

On a superficial level the most apparent contradiction is the one between a youthful passion for sensuality and energy and the weakness of old age. Celestina lost long ago the bloom which opened all doors and experienced all pleasures. She can only recover the joy of the body through the youth of others; and through wine, that is to say, through dream. But this need makes her dependent on them. Sempronio, at the end of the sinister dinner already described, cuts her pleasure short by telling her that she is an old woman and that they will now continue their games by themselves. She is torn by two opposed forces: her failing body which longs for repose and the immense energy required by her perpetual search for her lost youth. A more profound contradiction is entailed by the need to destroy ethical rules and social mores in order to subject her victims to her will. Let us look at Pármeno's case. He is a good young man and a loyal and faithful servant. Celestina must destroy the virtues which link him to his master Calisto, and replace them by a subjugation of his will to hers. She does this by subtly undermining the young man's self-esteem (by revealing to him that his mother was a witch) and by inflaming him with lust for Areusa. But, obviously, once the moral norm of loyalty to a master has been eliminated, there is no reason why Pármeno should be loyal to Celestina; in fact, he will encourage Sempronio to kill her, and both will be executed for their crime, so illustrating Rojas' thesis that in a diabolical world all are victims. Deprived of rules, we are left with fierce individuals dominated by obsessive, all-consuming passions. The only possible way in which these explosive egos can live together is through the unstable equilibrium created by temporary alliances of self-interest. In such a world, aging implies no redemption, no self-improvement.

In his book *Lautréamont et Sade,* Maurice Blanchot writes of the Sadean universe: "This philosophy (Sade's) has as its principle first self-interest; than total egoism. Everyone must seek his pleasure; there can be no other rule. This moral is then founded on the most absolute loneliness."[27] But Sade and Rojas part here: for Sade, this will to crime is the very source of joy; for Rojas, the source of all evil and of self-destruction. Rojas believes in Nature: old age is a natural stage of human life and must be accepted. Of necessity human passions must take into account time and the body; the energy of youth must grow into wisdom. But if our pride rejects the humiliation of organic withering, if it remains entangled in lust and greed, we shall be drawn irresistibly to an infernal circle of dependence upon others and of subjugation of them. We shall become prisoners of a dream and allies of the devil. This was the fatal mistake of the brilliant Celestina: trusting Satan, the master spider fell finally into his net.

3

MONTAIGNE'S FINAL REVISIONS: AN ERIKSONIAN ASSESSMENT

By Laurence M. Porter

[The private life of the author may be distinguished, although sometimes with difficulty, from the public (divulged) life of the narrator. It is likely, for example, that the author is more detached from society than is the self he portrays, by virtue of the fact that he, the author, is caught up in his writing. Meanwhile the at least partially transformed personage we meet in the narrative has more time for social intercourse. The historical author, that is, may well see himself as a gregarious and solidary fellow at those very moments when he is alone in his study describing the social details of his life. Can a writer dedicate himself to self-examination, and to sharing the fruits of that introspection with others through art, and still be successful in the real and private world of interpersonal relationships? Montaigne (like Proust) may be more sociable, more solidary, in his writings than in his life.

Is maturity to be assessed through an author's stance or on the basis of his or her underlying values? Is being parental a sign of maturity, as Erikson's concept of generativity might lead us to believe? The celebrated humanist uses his erudition to document his thoughts and to establish authority, hoping to make himself seem expert and wise in the company of ancient philosophers. But he also uses the seemingly detached discus-

sion of issues to establish his maturity and paternalness. Montaigne's more genuine movements toward maturity are to be found in his introspection, however. Well aware that self-disclosure is a key to his originality, Montaigne is secure enough to unveil his shortcomings in the name of solidarity. These include the ways in which he has not achieved full maturity. If Montaigne is a crypto-elitist, it's that he distinguishes himself—and knows it, of course—through the act of writing. It allows him, the perceptive, omniscient one who actually set pen to paper, to transcend the foibles of the likable chap inhabiting his pages—Eds.]

FOR GENERATIONS, critics have praised the wisdom of Michel de Montaigne, portraying his character as a model of self-fulfillment. His dedication to emotional adjustment and to self-realization has found many echoes in our psychologically-oriented century. The portrait of the omnicompetent, cosmopolitan "Renaissance Man" in Rudolph Burckhardt's classic *Civilization of the Renaissance in Italy* was modeled on Montaigne. The French philosopher managed to inspire the trust and respect of both sides during the bloody religious wars between Catholics and Reformed. He served two terms as mayor of the city of Bordeaux. Decades or even centuries before society acted in conformity to his recommendations, he advocated religious tolerance, progressive education, and the abolition of slavery and judicial torture. He maintained a precarious balance between philosophical skepticism, illustrated by his motto "What *do* I know?", and respect for established religious dogmas and legal and political institutions. He invoked Providence in discussing God's relations with us, and Fortune in discussing the material vicissitudes of human affairs. While winning approval from the highest ecclesiastical authorities, he elaborated the first detailed, essentially pagan self-portrait in modern Western literature, claiming that it reflected the image of all mankind. From this portrait original sin, guilt, prayer, grace, and redemption are lacking; it is a model of secular humanism.

Montaigne's intellectual development and the growth of his sense of solidarity are notable in the successive versions of his essays. Critics agree in finding a striking increase in self-disclosure, independence from classical and historical sources, and concern for others in his writings between 1578 and 1588. But they see the revisions of the last four years of his life as a sterile accumulation of quotations from classical authors, with erudite embellishment replacing personal inspiration. Pierre Villey remains the most influential exponent of this traditional view. He wrote that "the 1595 edition is scarcely more than a commentary on the 1588 edition." According to Villey, the 1595 edition suffers artistically from the insertion of disruptive digressions, excessive authorial self-consciousness, and massive insertions of Latin borrowings. He suggests that the sources of Montaigne's inspiration after 1588 are limited to the sum of his readings, with the distasteful exception that he seeks to affirm his originality by means of increasingly indiscreet confessions concerning his personal habits.[1] Later critics have not seriously challenged Villey. Donald Frame, the leading American critic, asserts that from 1588–92 "we find none of the major changes and developments that we have observed earlier," for Montaigne's mind "is now fully formed."[2]

Unlike Villey, Frame does not disparage the writings of Montaigne's last four years, but he lets stand the implication that these writings are devoid of interest. The unresolved question should be answered: did Montaigne, a model of humanistic wisdom, lose his capacity for original thinking toward the end of life, or did he continue a creative transformation of his earlier ideas? A psychological definition of successful aging is essential if we are to evaluate the achievement of Montaigne's last years.

The psychiatrist Erik Erikson divides life into eight stages, each with its appropriate task. The first four of these are a desexualized version of Freud's oral, anal, phallic, and genital stages of child development. The latter four are more original. Full adulthood, Erikson believes, is achieved in the seventh stage: the struggle between generativity and self-absorption. The person who achieves generativity develops the capacity to nurture future generations, to care for other people and things through child-rearing, work, the social responsibilities of maturity, and altruism. Then the final stage of life consists of a struggle between the temptations of despair and the drive toward ego-integrity. Retirement, the loss of loved ones, physical deterioration, and the threat of death can lead one to despair if life has seemed frustrating and too short: there are no second chances. Then one will wish that one's parents, one's life, and one's future might have been different. The resulting fear and self-contempt are masked typically by a generalized, querulous dissatisfaction with other people and with institutions—by chronic complaints. On the other hand, one can achieve integrity with the aid of the ego's accrued assurance of its proclivity for order and meaning. Then the aging person comes to accept his or her one and only life cycle as something that had to be and that contributes to the ongoing flow of life even as one steps aside for others. To acknowledge the inevitability of death can lead to a reassuring sense of one's place in the succession of generations. This awareness leads in turn to a new and different love of one's parents, to sympathy toward their role in one's life, and to a growing sense of solidarity with people in distant times and places and in occupations different from one's own. Such healthy renunciation robs death of its terrors. The aging person accepts the ultimate moral paternity of the self and continues to defend her or his autonomy against physical, social, and economic threats, in a harmonious blending of assertiveness and acceptance of the self as limited.[3]

After 1588, Montaigne expresses attitudes of generativity and integrity more frequently: he develops and deepens them. The essential test of his maturation after 1588 is to examine such statements in context, to see whether they modify the nature of Montaigne's ideas and the flow of his arguments, and if so, how. In their settings, the C-version or post-1588 passages show Montaigne focusing and consolidating his thought. Without introducing radical innovations during this period, Montaigne nevertheless transforms individual essays, particularly some of the earlier ones, by exploring anew the consequences of his mature viewpoint.

The major sources of C-additions[4] which reflect Montaigne's psychic evolution are the essays "Nos Affections s'emportent au delà de nous" (I, 3); "De l'Institution des enfants" (I, 26);

"De l'affection des pères aux enfants" (II, 8—a negative movement toward mistrust); "Apologie de Raimond Sebond" (II, 12); "De la praesumption" (II, 17); "D'un enfant monstrueux" (II, 30); "Du repentir" (III, 2); "De la vanité" (III, 9); and "De l'expérience" (III, 13).[5] All the essays, of course, preserve the early statements of their first two versions alongside the latest additions, so that each constitutes an intellectual and emotional autobiography.

Generally speaking, in the A-versions (to 1580) Montaigne searches historical accounts and the literature of classical antiquity to collect examples of behavior in critical social situations. In the B-versions (1580–88) he tends to disclose his own character and opinions. In the C-versions he continues to gather examples of behavior from other cultures and from classical authors, but now he uses them differently: to move his discussion to the plane of generality in such a way as to show solidarity with others. Thus the subsisting A-statements that "others do thus and so," which were originally opposed by the B-statements, "but I do otherwise," are subsumed into a tolerant synthesis in the C-statements: "given these differences between individuals, observe the humanness we share." The clearest example of this evolution appears in the two-page essay I, 13, "Cérémonie de l'entrevue des rois." It contains four movements of thought. (1) A-version: it is more courteous to remain in one's home to receive royalty, rather than going forth to greet them. You might miss them by seeking on the wrong road. (2) B-version: even at the risk of offending, I myself avoid all ceremony at home, for it is servitude. (3) A-version: some say the lesser-ranking person should arrive at a rendez-vous first; others say, after his superior. (4) C-version: "Not only every country, but also each city and profession has its peculiar forms of civility. . . . Etiquette ("la science de l'entregent") is a most useful study . . . for it opens the way for us to be instructed by the example of others" (p. 69). Here Montaigne characteristically moves in successive versions from the conventional to the withdrawn to the solidary—feeling kinship with people everywhere—although the latter remains on an intellectual plane rather than being translated into a will to action.

A C-version passage in "De l'expérience" demonstrates an Eriksonian solidarity with generations past and present by transforming the conventional Renaissance metaphor that we are like Pygmies sitting on the shoulders of the giants of classical antiquity, but that from there we can see farther than they. Montaigne's version of this image suggests a more intimate, organic connection: our opinions are grafted on each other like plants. "The first provides a stem for the second, the second for the third. Thus we climb upward rung by rung" (p. 1199).

Montaigne's humanistic solidarity does not appear for the first time in the C-version. He had already demonstrated a sense of affinity with persons from exotic cultures in the A and B-version of such essays as "Des cannibales" (I, 31); "Coutume de l'île de Céa" (II, 3); or "Des coches" (III, 6). He criticized his readers for presuming to look down on people from foreign lands who do not know the French language and customs, and who wear different clothes. Is human nature supposed to model itself on French ways? Indeed, we condemn everything which seems strange and incomprehensible to us (II, 12, pp. 515–516). Before 1588, however, Montaigne's thought betrays an element of contradiction in urging open-mindedness toward people from other cultures while expressing grave doubts about human understanding and intelligence in general. As he said in a B-version addition to "De la gloire" (II, 16, pp. 704–705), "the voice of the common herd is a source of ignorance, injustice and inconstance. . . . Let us constantly pursue reason; may public acclaim follow us that way if it will." In short, during the 1580's Montaigne came to respect the courage but not the opinions of ordinary folk. Intellectually he remained an elitist.

His elitism had early been attenuated in an A-variant of "De la praesumption": "there is no soul, however wretched and brutish it may be, in which one may not see some individual faculty shining" (p. 736). Such acceptance of people who are intellectually unprivileged and ungifted is extended to the physically deformed in the C-version of the brief essay II, 30, "D'un enfant monstrueux." It consists of only three paragraphs. The first, in the A-version, merely describes a Siamese twin with two bodies and one head as a curiosity whose survival symbolically offers hope for the survival of a France divided by religious strife. The second paragraph, added in the B-version, describes a grown man born without genitals but still enjoying physical contact with women. A C-version paragraph concludes the essay with a plea for broader-minded response to physical impairment. "What we call monsters are not such to God . . . We call things 'against nature' which are merely against custom. All things must be according to nature, whatever they be" (pp. 798–799). Thus in the late maturity of Montaigne, this essay evolved from a freakshow to a moral lesson. His changing attitude prepared him to accept as normal the universal physical deformations of illness, aging, and death.

But the ultimate in acceptance is to accept oneself. "Du repentir" states near the beginning that other authors communicate with their public through some external attribute foreign to their own essential identity, as if the latter were not worthy of attention. They write as grammarians, lawyers, or poets. "I am the first to communicate to a public through my universal being, as Michel de Montaigne" (p. 900). Of this Montaigne, nothing need be repressed, he now believes. A C-variant of "Sur des vers de Virgile" (III, 5) justifies Montaigne's "scandalous" disclosure of his sexual feelings and fantasies. "Each aspect of me is as much me as is any other. And no other makes me more a man in the strict sense of the word than this one" (p. 994). Self-acceptance appears even more unequivocally in a C-version passage of "De l'expérience." In it an animated dialogue welcomes and includes us as readers in a way that discursive writing does not. "I have done nothing today.—What, haven't you lived? That is not only the fundamental but also the most illustrious of your activities.—If I had been put in charge of great affairs, I would have shown what I can do.—Have you been able to reflect on and to shape your life? You have accomplished the greatest task of all . . . Our great and glorious masterpiece is living appropriately" (p. 1247). On the one hand, our fame and fortune should not deceive us, but on the other, the greatest of human aberrations is to scorn our own being (pp. 1257, 1250).

Montaigne personalized self-acceptance lucidly in a C-variant near the end of "Du repentir." "If I had to live over again, I would live again as I have before; I neither lament the past nor fear the future." After the harvest-time of life, he adds, he is entering the barren season—"Happily, because it is according to nature" (p. 913). Here Montaigne's statements correspond perfectly to Erikson's description of integrity. In contrast, the B-version passages of the concluding pages of this essay are filled with the vocabulary and imagery of struggle against an encroaching old age: the C-version expresses calm acceptance.

The self-contented person can give way for others. For example, the A-version of "Nos affections s'emportent au-delà de nous" (I, 3) begins with a series of picturesque tales of those who refused to die. Montaigne relates how dying military leaders arranged to continue symbolically fighting the enemy after their own demise—by being propped against a tree facing the opposing army, strapped to a horse which was then driven into battle against the foe, or by having a war drum made out of their skin. After 1588, Montaigne glosses these bald anecdotes by appending a tale concerning how some Athenian captains who stopped pursuing the enemy in order to recover their fallen comrades' bodies from the waves lost the chance for a decisive victory. It soon becomes apparent that this new story constitutes an indirect form of renunciation for the aging Montaigne, who contemplates his own death and does not wish artificially to prolong his presence, so to speak, beyond it. For the C-version then cites St. Augustine to the effect that burial, monuments, and funeral services are more a consolation for the living than a help to the dead. And it quotes Socrates replying "however you like" when Crito asked him how he wanted to be buried. In short, Montaigne vicariously yields to the wishes of posterity and eschews the temptation of the dead appealing to the living.

Montaigne's earliest essays like "Que philosopher c'est apprendre à mourir" already urge us to "make way for others, as others have done for you" (I, 20, p. 119). But a C-version passage in this same essay translates abstract recognition into a plan of action:

> At this hour I am in such a state, thanks to God, that I can depart when it pleases Him, without regretting anything unless it be life itself, should its loss weigh on me. I am detaching myself on all sides; I have halfway taken my leave of everyone, save myself. Never did a man prepare himself to leave the world more purely and fully, nor did he release it more universally than I expect to do (pp. 112–113).

Two further C-additions here link renunciation to solidarity, first by stressing the democracy of the body: when Socrates was told that the thirty tyrants of Athens had condemned him to death, he replied, "and nature has condemned them" (p. 116). And toward the end of the essay, still with regard to death, Montaigne sums up saying "equality is the first condition for equity. Who can complain of being included where all are included?" (p. 119).

Renunciation and self-acceptance merge in essay III, 10, "De ménager sa volonté." Already in the B-version, Montaigne says: "I am no longer capable of great changes . . . In brief, I am involved in completing this man, rather than in remaking another" (pp. 1132–1133). But the C-version triples the length of this development, with the second-longest addition to the essay after 1588. The longest addition follows shortly. There Montaigne implicitly defends himself against the criticism made at the papal court that he had tolerated heresy by mentioning in print the Huguenot poet Théodore de Bèze (pp. 1135–1137). The first of these two long additions means that Montaigne agrees passing time is leaving him behind. He must renounce an active role in life. The second addition shows that he will not therefore renounce his judgment in esthetic matters. To retire does not necessitate forfeiting one's integrity.

The one occasion when Montaigne's tranquil self-control obviously breaks down is in "De l'affection des pères aux enfants" (II, 8). There he fears a helpless old age because he mistrusts those close to him. This time the B-version is more optimistic than the C. It states that old age suffers from so many shortcomings and incapacities that commands and intimidation no longer are appropriate weapons; one's only protection is to try to inspire confidence. As a counter-example Montaigne imagines a miserly old man pillaged behind his back by all his household. The C-version develops and generalizes this scene in picturesque detail. Old people's senses become so dim that they are easily tricked. Montaigne adds that he is very gullible himself. He says wistfully that a disinterested friend is a treasure in comparison to legally-enforced relationships with unreliable family members. And he admits that whenever he hears a story about an old man duped by those he trusts, he applies it to himself, suspiciously testing whether he is not being tricked in the same manner (pp. 432–434). In this painful situation, Montaigne mistrusts his own judgment as well: a C-addition urges distributing one's estate according to the customs of the land rather than by personal caprice near the end of life (pp. 437–438). "De l'affection des pères aux enfants" does exceptionally betray Montaigne's wish that his family and servants were different,[6] whereas in Eriksonian terms full self-acceptance includes the acceptance of others in one's life, despite all their shortcomings.[7]

In short, Montaigne succeeds intellectually in facing death and experiencing a common bond with others,[8] but he does not always achieve such maturity in emotional and practical terms. To do so, perhaps, would be superhuman. In any event, Montaigne's *Essais* mainly evade the problem of dealing with his household by not talking about them; and by letting established law determine his legacy, he obviates emotional commitment. Working within the system in politics, religion, and family life, he avoids disruptive crises of conscience. In other areas, the development of his essays and their growing fame generates in him a sense of personal uniqueness and achievement. Such self-awareness leads to greater emotional flexibility than in Montaigne's early career as a writer, because he need no longer define himself in opposition to death. It leads to greater solidarity as well because he need no longer define himself physically and morally in opposition to others. Intellectually he remains a crypto-elitist, as his erudite compilations reveal, but this pride does not prevent him from yielding gracefully to the generations to come.

4

KING LEAR AND THE CRISIS OF RETIREMENT

By Laurel Porter

[Shakespeare looks for growth in age and meaning in madness. Modern humanistic psychology attempts to see altered states of consciousness such as madness and hallucinations as meaningful, perhaps even growth-inducing, experiences. It would be unfair to the richness of the work, however, to make a simple distinction between "reason" and "madness" while overvaluing the latter. Critics have addressed the lucidity of madness in King Lear *in that way. It is more accurate to say that a psychotic* episode *is instrumental in modifying the king's neurotic traits. The value of Lear's experience of madness is in the sense which he can make of it later as an integrated person, rather than for any inherent meaning. The same may be said of Lear's aging. He does not become wise just because he is old, but he is able to use the calamities of his final developmental crisis to become a vastly different person and a better parent. The following chapter examines that development—Eds.]*

MUCH HAS BEEN MADE of intergenerational problems, and especially of father-daughter relationships, in Shakespeare. *King Lear* lends itself particularly well to the analysis of family relationships because of the obvious strife between Lear and his daughters. But the painful conflict between generations which many feel to be central to the tragedy of *King Lear* is merely the most striking symptom of a larger problem, that of Lear's retirement. He relinquishes all of his land but fails to accept the resulting loss of power. Two of his daughters abuse their inheritance shamefully, but I see in the play a developmental problem of the aging adult where other critics have commented solely on the more striking father-daughter hostilities, or on socio-political issues, such as Lear's obligation to hold Britain together by staying on the throne.

Some critics feel that Lear's retirement is wrong in and of itself, basically because it tragically disturbs the Elizabethan concept of order.[1] The King's right to retire is usually not acknowledged. As he says,

> 'Tis our fast intent
> To shake all cares and business from our age,
> Conferring them on younger strengths while we
> Unburdened crawl toward death (I, i, 38–41).

This is a perfectly acceptable, ordinary wish for an octogenarian. In the natural course of things, many reach a moment when "cares and business" no longer fascinate and rest is desired. Yet at the same time, retirement from normal daily activities can be traumatic, even when it is voluntary, as it is here. For many, retirement signals that one is officially old, or worse, officially useless. Lear's loss of kingly power is a metaphor for the loss of physical and mental powers in old age generally. The real test of the King is whether or not he can adjust to his own decision to relinquish power. His ability to accept his own aging process has more to do with his relationship to himself than with his relationship to his daughters. In my point of view it is not the abdication itself which throws order into chaos, but Lear's mishandling of it, due to his ambivalence about retiring.

The abdication is the central event of the play's opening. Lear demands vows of absolute devotion from his daughters. Instead of dividing the kingdom equally among the three as an inheritance gained by *birthright,* he sets up a deadly competition whereby their portion must be earned as a *reward.* The rivalry which Lear thereby encourages among his daughters will account for the deaths of all three.

Regan and Goneril fall into the bitter contest immediately. Their competitiveness disguised beneath a thin veneer of politeness, they vie aggressively; Goneril proclaims hypocritically, "I love you/As much as child e'er loved, or father found," to which Regan counters:

> I am made
> Of that self metal as my sister,
> And prize me at her worth. In my true heart
> I find she names my very deed of love,
> Only she comes too short . . . (I, i, 72–76).

In this attempt to outdo her sister, Regan unwittingly reveals the nature of her valuation of her father by stating her case in material terms. The language she uses—metal, prize, worth, and deed—evokes money and legal documents.

But the youngest, Cordelia, refuses to enter the competition. Lear attempts to draw her into it by asking, "what can you say to draw/A third more opulent than your sisters?" Her answer—"Nothing"—throws the King into a rage. He immediately disowns and banishes her. The violence of his reaction to her reply may be understood in terms of his neurotic needs and unreasonable expectations. Lear has been King for a long, long time; he is an imperious monarch accustomed to commanding absolute obedience. Because he confuses obedience with love, he takes her words as an utter rejection.

Of course, Cordelia—the one unhypocritical daughter—is not rejecting her father; she is merely refusing to claim that she loves him better than she does. Two suitors are courting Cordelia, and she refuses to promise greater love to her father than to her future husband:

> Good my lord,
> You have begot me, bred me, loved me; I
> Return those duties back as are right fit,
> Obey you, love you, and most honor you.
> Why have my sisters husbands, if they say
> They love you all? Happily, when I shall wed,
> That lord whose hand must take my plight shall carry
> Half my love with him, half my care and duty.
> Sure I shall never marry like my sisters,
> To love my father all (I, i, 101–110).

Lear makes himself appear ludicrous in the eyes of Goneril and Regan and even of Kent when he banishes Cordelia for her chaste "nothing," and he undermines his position as a respected authority figure by his insistence upon unquestioning obedience after the abdication. Certainly Lear merits the respect due to a former monarch, but he continues to expect absolute obedience. This is unreasonable. He includes a clause in the abdication agreement whereby he maintains the title of King after passing power and property on to his children, thereby reserving the rights of kingship while relinquishing its responsibilities. "The King would speak with Cornwall," he commands regally when he is no longer King (II, iv, 110). He steps down voluntarily in the knowledge that his powers are beginning to fail, but he is in fact unwilling to cease being King.

Why is Lear unable or unwilling truly to abdicate? Is it senility, decrepitude? I think not. At the time of Shakespeare's writing, of course, the tale of the impetuous old king had been familiar for centuries; the rashness of the legendary Lear was associated with his advanced age long before Shakespeare wrote the play. But Shakespeare's rich treatment of Lear's character does not limit itself to age stereotypes. The flaws which prevent the King from abdicating fully are more related to his personality than to senescence;[2] he is unable to abdicate because his self-concept depends on others' obedience to him. The extent to which age is a factor in Lear's overreactions is unclear in the play, but Goneril's view rings true: age has only aggravated his existing faults; "The best and soundest of his time hath been but rash; then must we look to receive, not alone the imperfections of long-engraffed condition, but therewithal the unruly waywardness that infirm and choleric years bring with them" (I, i, 324–328).

Lear's is, apparently, a long-standing insensitivity. His preference for Cordelia, obvious from the outset of the play, embittered the two wicked sisters with jealousy. Goneril says to Regan, "He always loved our sister most" (I, i, 319–320). His impulsiveness, and his confusion between love and obedience, probably contributed to making monsters of two of his three daughters. In addition to his preoccupation with himself which blinds him to the emotional needs of his daughters, his unreflective wielding of power alienates those who would in normal circumstances have been the comfort of his old age.

Critics have written on both sides of the question of Lear's physical and mental competence. G. B. Harrison writes unequivocally, "The tragedy of Lear is that he brings his suffering on his own head by a grievous stupidity" [and] "understands neither himself nor his daughters . . . Lear's fault is a fault of the mind, a mind unwarrantably, because selfishly, foolish."[3] And Derek Traversi goes so far as to say that "old age has weakened his capacity for self-control."[4] Even the loyal Kent speaks of "this hideous rashness" in reference to Lear's disinheritance of Cordelia, the only daughter who does not in fact forsake him. Lear's decision to disown Cordelia is a fatal error, for Goneril and Regan will not even give him shelter. They fear that their father's banishment of Cordelia and of Kent is a harbinger of future, even more erratic, behavior. They would like to divest Lear of the power to go back on his decisions in their favor, and are desperate to discredit Lear before he realizes his error in trusting them; Goneril's urgent "We must do something, and i' the heat" is the last line of Act One, Scene One.

It will suit Goneril's needs to insist on Lear's "dotage." Her claim of his encroaching senility is intended to undermine his credibility in her husband's eyes, for instance. She finds it easier to deal with her difficult father by branding him as senile than to confront him directly on her real fear that he may turn against her and take back the wealth which he has given her. She implies that Lear is deluded in his wish to retain his knights (actually a prudent provision for political protection on Lear's part) on the grounds that they are riotous and that he is unable to discipline them. She is functioning not only as Lear's bitter and insecure daughter, but also as his political enemy, and is guiltily paranoid about Lear's train:

> A hundred knights?
> 'Tis politic and safe to let him keep
> At point a hundred knights; yes, that on every dream,
> Each buzz, each fancy, each complaint, dislike,
> He may enguard his dotage with their powers
> And hold our lives in mercy (I, iv, 328–334).

To maintain power over the King, Goneril plans to unite with Regan in treating him disrespectfully. In this way he will be humiliated. She hopes to take advantage of his age, reasoning that he must be corrected like a child: "Now, by my life, old fools are babes again" (I, iv, 14–20).

Goneril succeeds in shaking Lear's self-confidence, but her mistreatment of him also incites him to see things as they truly are; he soon realizes his error in giving away all his power and property to her and Regan. He is hesitant to blame Goneril for her behavior, however, because he is beginning to realize that he has already treated one daughter—Cordelia—unfairly. He is now aware of having been suspicious and unfair, and is beginning to be concerned that problems between him and his children might be partially his own fault. This constitutes an important step in Lear's understanding of himself and of human relationships.

Once he is certain of Goneril's disrespect, however, he proves to be no less rash than before. In a terrible speech, he damns her to sterility or to unbearable torture at the hands of her own offspring. He is horrified that such a monster as she could be the issue either of him or of his late wife. "Are you our daughter?" he asks her mockingly (I, iv, 215); a question not confused or senile, but sarcastic.

Lear leaves Goneril's palace for Regan's, little knowing that Goneril has warned Regan to refuse, also, to entertain him. En route, the Fool chides Lear in riddles; "If thou wert my fool, nuncle, I'd have thee beaten for being old before thy time" (I, v, 38–39). "Thou shouldst not have been old till thou hadst been wise" (I, v, 41–42). There is truth here, for had Lear been wise, he would have passed on the property—and power—to all three sisters; the faithful Cordelia and her honorable new husband, the King of France, would have entertained the retired monarch as befitted him, and they would have been a powerful ally with him against any coup d'état on the part of the other two sisters. The realization of his error, and of what might have been, is deeply disturbing to Lear. In this scene (I, v), wherein he says, "I did her wrong" (presumably speaking of Cordelia) Lear recognizes the possibility of losing his mind.

In Act Two, Scene One, Regan and her husband, the Duke of Cornwall, go to the Earl of Gloucester's castle in order to turn Gloucester against Lear, and in order to be away when

Lear arrives at their palace to seek shelter; we know that this visit is more truly an absence from home than a presence at Gloucester's: "I have this present evening from my sister/Been well informed of them, and with such cautions/That, if they come to sojourn at my house, I'll not be there" (II, i, 108–111).

Further humiliations of the King are to come in Scene Two of the second act. Lear's aide, the disguised Earl of Kent, meets Oswald, Goneril's steward, who is carrying a message against the King. Kent insults Oswald, who was rude to the King in an earlier scene, and in wonderful detail. Cornwall has Kent put in the stocks for this verbal abuse of the insolent messenger-boy—an unthinkable offense to the King. Everything in this scene is intended to underscore Lear's loss of status. Cornwall decrees that Kent shall be stocked until noon, but Regan pushes further: "Till noon? Till night, my lord, and all night too!" Kent says to her, "Why, madam, if I were your father's dog,/You should not use me so," to which she retorts, "Being his knave, I will" (II, ii, 137–140). Gloucester asks Cornwall not to stock Kent, pointing out that such punishment is reserved for the most common of pilferers, but he is completely ineffectual. The indignity of finding his messenger in the stocks will be a major humiliation for Lear.

Interestingly, Oswald claims that he spared Kent's life on account of his "grey beard." Cornwall, too, refers to Kent's age, saying, "What, art thou mad, old fellow?" Goneril had used age to undermine Lear's credibility and Cornwall does the same thing here with Kent. But this labeling with regard to years is highly arbitrary since, although Lear is eighty, Kent is only forty-eight years old. Kent explains to Cornwall that he serves the King, but this carries no weight with the power-hungry Cornwall, for the King is King no longer. Kent, in speaking with the boldness of the King's representative, is living in the past, as is Lear. He unrealistically (although justifiably) expects that Lear's daughters and their husbands will continue to honor the King; it is not age, but an uninformed view of the ambitious and avaricious people around them which takes both Lear and Kent off guard. Nor is it age per se, but rather the loss of power involved in Lear's retirement, which creates Lear's vulnerability. The significance of his advanced age is becoming clearer; for Lear it means a certain weariness and the desire to retire to the comfort of his daughters' care; for Goneril, Regan and Cornwall, it represents a pretext for claiming that he is incompetent, an opportunity for seizing power.

Outside the gates of Gloucester's castle, Lear arrives after finding Regan absent from home. Deeply shocked to find Kent in the stocks, he nonetheless resists the thought that Regan has become as inhospitable as Goneril; he is pathetically unwilling to believe that he has lost her love and respect. At the same time, her cruelty grows sharper. Gloucester is intimidated by Cornwall. "You know the fiery quality of the Duke," he lamely says to Lear, who flies into a rage of frustration and incomprehension. Yet despite the outrage, Lear decides to reserve judgment. "May be he is not well," he says to excuse his son-in-law. In spite of the stocking of Kent and the delay in Regan's arrival, Lear greets Regan eagerly. When he begins to complain of Goneril's actions, however, Regan clarifies her position. She says flatly,

> O, sir, you are old!
> Nature in you stands on the very verge
> Of her confine. You should be ruled, and led
> By some discretion that discerns your state
> Better than you yourself. Therefore I pray you
> That to our sister you do make return;
> Say you have wronged her (II, iv, 160–166).

So Regan chooses, along with Goneril, cruelly to humiliate her father and to treat him as senile rather than to express her anger more directly by confronting him on his tyrannical habits. Yet even after this speech, Lear wants to believe that Regan will entertain and comfort him, and that she will welcome his train. While this is unrealistic, it shows Lear's mighty effort to control himself, to reserve judgment. He is making every attempt not to repeat the mistakes of the past.

But Goneril enters, and Lear is outraged by her arrival. He is distressed to see that Regan takes her by the hand, a pointed sign that the two are allied. Goneril again refers disparagingly to Lear's "dotage" and Regan informs her father that he must return to Goneril, since she is unable to entertain him herself: "I am now from home, and out of that provision/Which shall be needful for your entertainment" (II, iv, 231–232). This excuse is so weak that it may be understood as an affront. She stipulates the diminution of the king's train from 100 to fifty, but Lear does not seem to take note. In a supreme effort to control himself, he tells Goneril that he'll not chide her. He is still trying to believe that he can stay with Regan, along with his hundred knights. By the end of the scene, Goneril and Regan have agreed that Lear will not need any knights whatsoever. Lear cries out that patience is what he truly needs. He is bitterly aware of the imminent danger of going mad. In structural parallel to the King's state of mind, a storm begins to rage without. Lear runs out into the tempest, and Gloucester is persuaded to bolt the doors of his castle as Act Two comes to a close.

On the heath, Kent discovers Lear in high rage. The King curses all fertility, since ungrateful children are born—a regression from generativity. His rage results largely from the frustration of being rejected by his daughters despite his munificence, and at precisely the moment when he is trying most earnestly to mend his ways. The strains involved in repressing his anger at the daughters who have acted so spitefully is too great. "My wits begin to turn," he announces with frightening lucidity.

An ironic cycle of cause and effect is at play: Lear has been tyrannical both as monarch and as parent, but he has reached a point of being willing to give up most of his power and much of his pomp in exchange for love, respect, comfort and care; he was reaching a certain measure of integrity in being able to pass on most of his land and authority to his children. However, two of the daughters received all he gave them only to shun and bitterly humiliate him. Their hatred may have been caused by his always having ruled them instead of loving them, and because he favored Cordelia, but they are unable to forgive him even when he shows that he is willing to change. And when he acknowledges his error in banishing Cordelia, and is on the verge of learning humility, his growth is temporarily hampered by the violence of his daughters' rejection. Goneril and Regan shame him deeply, and then a lightning storm threatens his life. Lear's episode of madness is the result of an extraordinary set of circumstances orchestrated by Shakespeare to achieve the most devastating effect; but out of that experience the King will emerge curiously enlightened. For one thing, Lear develops a social conscience, a certain solidarity with mankind. Exposed to the elements, Lear is humbled as he shares, for the first time, the plight of his miserable subjects. He realizes that the poor suffer, exclaiming, "Oh, I have ta'en too little care of this!/Take physic, pomp;/ Expose thyself to feel what wretches feel . . . " (III, iv, 39–41).

Lear is not able to think reasonably during much of the storm, but he is able to vent his anger. Shakespeare plays with the characters' sense of reality during the tempest. The thunder makes it difficult to hear. The rain obscures vision—Gloucester does not recognize Lear at first, or his own son, Edgar. Lightning illuminates the scene for dramatic effect. Both Kent and Edgar are in disguise, and Lear's and Gloucester's failure to recognize them is symbolic of their more general blindness. Gloucester attempts to reason with the King, but Lear finds more insight in his exposure to the storm and in seemingly nonsensical banter. His madness is an altered state of consciousness more rich in insights than is his usual state of mind. He intensifies the split between reality and delusion, and is able to express his outrage, by convening a carnavalesque "court" for putting his daughters on trial, with the disguised Edgar, the disguised Kent, and the Fool as participants.

Disguised as a mad beggar, "Poor Tom", Edgar (Gloucester's mistreated son) plays an important part in helping the King to work through his rage. When Lear sees Edgar as "Poor Tom," his first reaction is to say, "Didst thou give all to thy two daughters. And art thou come to this?" Kent's attempt at reality orientation ("He hath no daughter, sir") fails to distract Lear from his preoccupation (III, iv). But the King is astonished and inspired by the naked madman. Here man is stripped to his miserable hide, exposed to bitter weather. Lear begins to contemplate when it means to be human. "Thou are the thing itself; unaccommodated man is no more but such a poor, bare, forked animal as thou art" (III, iv, 111–113). He proceeds to tear off his own clothes, as if to demonstrate that he, the King, is as little—and as much—a man as "Poor Tom." Edgar (as

"Tom") and the Fool encourage Lear's sense of unreality with nonsense talk in this scene, for they sense that the King needs an imaginative escape from unbearable reality.[5] Edgar pretends to see devils and the Fool blathers playfully in rhyme, while Lear imagines a thousand fiends attacking Regan and Goneril with fire. This flight into madness, facilitated by Edgar and the Fool, permits the politically vulnerable King to regress and to cry the full depth of his rage in safe company.

As Regan's and Goneril's crimes are compounded and the play fills with gore, and as Lear's personality changes, the audience feels more and more sympathy for the repentant King, whom Cordelia plans to rescue. Wearing a garland of wild flowers—a sort of nature's parody of a crown, befitting his newfound humility—he is less mad than he appears. There is much lucidity in his speech: "They told me I was everything. 'Tis a lie—I am not ague-proof" (IV, vi, 119–120). When the blinded Gloucester recognizes his voice and asks, "Is't not the King?" Lear replies, "Ay, every inch a king!" (IV, vi, 122–123). His sense of identity is clear now; he is not everything, but he is a king in a sense. The humanizing effect of his psychotic episode creates a partial resolution of the tragic conflict between Lear the King and Lear the man. Only after he comes to terms with himself as a fellow of other human beings will his reunion with Cordelia and their mutual forgiveness be possible.

Cordelia eventually succeeds in rescuing her father, who is now sleeping under a doctor's care. Music is played to awaken him gently, a striking contrast with his treatment at the hands of his other daughters and with the violence of the storm. Cordelia fears that the King is still out of his wits when he awakens, for he takes her for a spirit at first. He can scarcely believe that he is alive, let alone in the care of Cordelia, and is mistrustful of his senses;

> I am a very foolish fond old man,
> Fourscore and upward, not an hour more nor less;
> And to deal plainly,
> I fear I am not in my perfect mind. . . .
> Do not laugh at me;
> For (as I am a man) I think this lady
> To be my child Cordelia (IV, vii, 69–79).

Cordelia responds to her father with tender forgiveness. Lear has emerged from his developmental crisis fond and humble. It is difficult at this point in the play to say whether his spirit has been broken or whether, with new wisdom, he has transcended the avarice and hostility surrounding him. One thing is certain as Act Four closes: his rage has left him.

But Cordelia's French army loses the battle against her sisters' forces and she and her father are taken prisoners. In a beautiful speech which signals Lear's expanded capacity to enjoy human relationships, he says to Cordelia,

> We two alone will sing like birds i' the cage,
> When thou dost ask me blessing, I'll kneel down
> And ask of thee forgiveness (V, iii, 10–12).

He is thinking about the quality of time spent with a loved one for the first time in the play. The sole presence of Cordelia is important to him now, and he is able to savor her brief visit.

The King displays in this same speech a certain detachment from daily events. He is disengaging from his role as monarch while strengthening his identity as a man and as a father. Instead of attempting to involve himself in the deadly power struggle in which Edmund, Goneril and Regan are still engaged, Lear is content to retire to his prison cell, to reminisce ("tell old tales") and to consider the ins and outs of courtly life with bemused detachment. This is what retirement can afford: a time for evaluating the meaning of one's life, "And take upon's the mystery of things,/As if we were God's spies" (V, iii, 17–18). He can engage in reminiscence and life review only in the comforting presence of Cordelia. But she is killed, and Lear never has the opportunity to take stock of what his life has meant. Therein, I suspect, lies the real tragedy of *King Lear*.

Although Lear swings at moments from regal to puerile, from lucid to confused, and from towering to fallen, he progresses more generally from a state of insensitivity and self-absorption to a solidarity with mankind and an ability to share love. This growth, which occurs despite long years of absolute control over others, is catalyzed by a series of abuses involved in his retirement and in his own failure to relinquish power. In a slow and painful process of trial and error, Lear learns the real differences between his two elder daughters and Cordelia, and begins to recognize his own faults. When he does so it is very late, but not too late for him and Cordelia to express forgiveness. Instead of playing the King with her, he finally accepts to be her father and simply to enjoy her companionship. If Lear is slow to adapt to the loss of power accompanying his retirement from office, his spiritual triumph is that he finally attains integrity. He learns to value loyality over power and love over obedience, and comes to see himself as a person worthy of affection. This is all to the good.

But to "speak what we feel, not what we ought to say," the play ends dismally, with little to redeem the events which have passed. Goneril, Regan, Edmund, Gloucester, Cordelia and King Lear die. Edmund had said earlier, "The younger rises when the old doth fall" (III, iv, 24). Yet the few survivors are left in sorry circumstances when the King dies. Kent is about to die of a broken heart. There is no clear sense of who should become the leader. None of those who remain can know the richness of human experience which was King Lear's: "The oldest hath borne most; we that are young/Shall never see so much, nor live so long" (V, iii, 391–392).

5

BALZAC'S MYTH OF REJUVENATION

By Eugene F. Gray

[Focusing on Balzac, but with references ranging from the ancient Babylonian Epic of Gilgamesh *to the present, Professor Gray explores the forms and meanings of the perennial fantasy of miraculous longevity. The notion of an elixir of immortality, a fountain of youth, or a prolongation of life through draining the vital forces of young victims is not confined to legend or to melodrama. Goethe's Faust, for example, imbibes a magic potion and is rejuvenated by thirty years. In France, England, and Germany, early nineteenth-century preoccupation with pseudo-sciences such as Mesmerism encouraged a wave of speculation concerning the possibilities for human rejuvenation, and a plethora of vampire stories.* La Peau de Chagrin (The Wild Ass's Skin) *constitutes Balzac's chief fable of the life force consumed by the exercise of the will. Eugene Gray, an experienced Balzacian, traces the motif through many of Balzac's works.*

Balzac sees stresses as arising from civilization and its discontents, but in a sense opposite to that of Freud. Freud believed that the achievement of civilization inevitably involved the repression of our instincts and resultant frustration. (Or as Diderot put it in the eighteenth century, without law and order every young man would kill his father and sleep with his mother). Balzac, however, believed that civilization, particularly in the corrupting atmosphere of cities, exposed people to new needs and desires which would not have occurred to them in another setting. Striving to gratify these desires depletes one's supply of vital energy and leads to a premature death. To live long, the best recipe is to retreat to the country, or to a monk's or scholar's cell. Money serves Balzac as a metaphor for limited reserves of vital energy. Crooked financiers and usurers are the vampires of modern times. Hoarding of material possessions expresses our vain hope of immortality. A sublimated version of that hope is the myth of salvation through art. Fame will preserve our memory in the minds of men.

Such obsessions with the temporal prolongation of life, Gray suggests, are associated in Balzac with what one could call the spatial extension of life, through acquiring knowledge of all the discoveries and all the societies of the globe. If acquired through tranquil study, such knowledge would not exhaust the organism. But Balzac's own visionary powers as an imaginative and realistic writer—he claimed the ability to intuit the secrets of any human drama taking place near him in Paris, and he strove to sum up French social history for the entire first half of the nineteenth century—were achieved, in his view, only through the lavish expenditure of his reserves of "vital fluid," which were non-renewable. For himself, he chose the short, intense life over the long. Like Thomas Wolfe, he wrote himself to death. Thence his fascination with the road not taken—Eds.]

OF ALL THE MYRIAD ASPECTS of human existence of which primitive myth attempts to make sense, none is more universal nor more immediate than the fact that human beings are born, mature, age and finally and inevitably die. And while some people of course live longer than others, a distinct and envied few live an unusually long time, luckily avoiding the innumerable accidents and fatal diseases which traditionally have been the primary causes of death since the dawn of humanity. Those who manage to survive significantly beyond the proverbial allotment of three score and ten excite admiration among their contemporaries and survivors. While it must be admitted that most cases of extreme longevity lack sufficient documentation to convince the skeptical mind, it would appear that they are becoming rarer with the spread of modern record-keeping. Cases such as the Biblical Methuselah, who allegedly lived to the age of 969 years, are recognized by moderns as the stuff of legend, and even those who accept the literal truths of the old myths often admit that such events occurred in a distant, magical past.

The ancient Greeks, whose myths have played such an influential role in Western culture, believed that the earliest men enjoyed a long-lived existence, free of toil, pain and the ravages of old age. Death for these inhabitants of the Golden Age was no more than peaceful sleep, after which they became beneficent spirits. Subsequent generations, however, because of their wickedness, brought upon themselves divine wrath, resulting in mankind's affliction with the ills contained in Pandora's jar, among which was subjection to the process of senescence, whose end point is death. The Greek myth of the three Fates (the Moirae) illustrates in vivid fashion one popular conception: Clotho spins out the thread of life, Lachesis measures it, and Atropos snips the thread at death. Some traditions maintain that the three Fates were the parthenogenic daughters of Necessity, the "Strong Fate," which suggests the ineluctible nature of individual destiny.

Of particular interest in the Greek myth of mortality with respect both to Balzac's work and to modern views on aging is the hint of a natural upper limit to the human life span. Already in Genesis 6:3 the upper limit was set at one hundred twenty years, and in all suitably documented cases of extreme old age, the limit for the human species seems to be about 110–120 years.[1] In addition modern research, carried out by Leonard Hayflick and others, indicates that this limit has its roots in the cell itself. Normal human cells, whether grown *in vivo* or *in vitro,* will divide only about fifty times, at which point mitosis ceases.[2] Humankind's destiny is in its physiology.

Faced with the image of mortality represented above, one can choose an attitude of Job-like resignation. But myth and literature teem with examples of heroes striving to cheat death, to prolong or resuscitate life. Such is the subject of the ancient *Sumerian Epic of Gilgamesh,* dating from the third millenium B.C. But the eponymous hero Gilgamesh, after having found Utnapishtim, the one mortal to have earned immortality from the gods, fails the test put to him, and must return home as mortal as when he had left. However heroic they may be, those who follow the earliest generations of men rarely win immortality on earth—transcendence is generally the only path available.

Even in modern times the dream of conquering death persists, from Cyrano de Bergerac's seventeenth-century tales of immortal and quasi-immortal extraterrestrial beings, to Mary Shelley's celebration of new life in *Frankenstein,* to present-day attempts at preserving the body by freezing it until some future age when the maladies causing death will presumably have a cure. The common thread linking these latter-day dreams is faith in science, which provided Honoré de Balzac (1799–1850) with his primary inspiration. Indeed, the vast collection of novels, tales, stories and essays collected under the general title of *La Comédie humaine* was intended as a comprehensive study of modern society, on the model of contemporary biological studies, but in which social species replaced zoological species. Longevity is merely one trait among many peculiar to a species.

In Balzac's case, however, the concern with longevity has a greater function, comprising an important part of his creative imagination and often taking on the dimensions of myth. His interest in the subject undoubtedly stemmed originally from his father's obsession with remaining young. The elder Balzac prided himself on his excellent health, so certain of becoming a centenarian that he invested a large sum of money in a tontine, a type of investment trust (some would say a lottery) in which the investors left their money after their death such that the last surviving member became the sole beneficiary. (Monsieur Balzac senior unfortunately neither became a centenarian nor won the tontine, dying in 1829 at the age of 83.) Like modern advocates of good health, Bernard-François de Balzac (he added the "noble particle" in about 1821, although of southern peasant extraction) was moderate in his habits, watched his diet and exercised regularly, a regimen which the young Honoré himself did not follow, content to attribute it to some of his fictional characters.

An echo of the father's concern for good health appears in Honoré's "Traité des excitants modernes" ("Treatise on Modern Stimulants"), in which the author lists their deleterious effects. In Balzac's view the human body possesses a certain quantity of vital force which must be distributed among the various organs in order for good health to be maintained. Once this balance is disturbed, as is the tendency in the modern drive for pleasure, damage to the system results. "The excess of tobacco," he wrote, "the excess of coffee, the excess of opium and spirits produce serious disorders, and lead to an early death."[3] Such excesses can even debilitate an entire people, as Balzac maintained happened to the Dutch and the Turks because of their abuse of tobacco (XII, 325).

"Le Traité des excitants modernes," important as it is in Balzac's thought, does not go beyond a discussion of the external causes of accelerated aging. The remedy, sobriety, is within the reach of everyone, and permits one to reach a normal life span. But Balzac was intrigued by stories of those who have somehow cheated death, either prolonging their life significantly beyond the normal life span, or by returning from the dead. An early example is the fantastic tale of 1822 called *Le Centenaire, ou les deux Béringheld (The Centenarian, or the Two Béringhelds)*, a rather amateurish imitation of Maturin's *Melmoth the Wanderer*. Written under the pseudonym Horace de Saint-Aubin, *Le Centenaire* is fairly typical of the horror stories so popular during the early years of the nineteenth century. The eponymous protagonists are a young man named Tullius Béringheld, who rises to the rank of general in Napoleon's army, and his still-living ancestor, born in 1450 (and thus well over 350 years old at the end of the novel!).

How has the centenarian managed to prolong his life so radically? Contrary to the common method used in this type of story, it has not been by supernatural means, but by means of science. Now in using this word one must realize that Balzac's conception of science was not, could scarcely have been, the twentieth-century conception. In an age when chemistry was just beginning to distinguish itself from alchemy, it is not surprising to see a layman like Balzac accord equal faith to both, and adopt a basically vitalist point of view with regard to human life. Vitalism maintained that the difference between living and non-living things derived from a vital substance present in the former and lacking in the latter, whether it be in the blood or in the breath. The legend of Dracula is a macabre illustration of the vitalist point of view. Balzac's centenarian is a vampire of sorts, prolonging his life by extracting the vital fluid from the breath of his young victims. Approaching the time of renewal, the centenarian says to his last victim: "I feel already that I am having trouble forming my ideas, I am losing my vital fluid."[4] Earlier he had asked: "Since you wanted to die anyway, isn't it better that your breath extend my life?" (IV, 186).

The centenarian's lair, hidden within the catacombs beneath the city of Paris, has the typical décor of the Gothic tale: human skulls lying on a table, skeletons, strange metal instruments, old parchments covered with arcane writing, and the like (IV, 172). Balzac does not describe in detail the scientific instruments used by the centenarian, or hazard a theory about how the centenarian extracts the vital fluid from his victim's breath: Balzac does not have the technical turn of mind of a modern writer of science fiction.

The antechamber to the centenarian's lair is a storehouse of ancient bric-a-brac: fragments of Joan of Arc's funeral pyre, stones from the Bastille, Ravaillac's skull (i.e. the assassin of Henri IV), Cromwell's Bible, Charles IX's arquebus, Christopher Columbus' globe. These are the material counterparts to the storehouse of erudition which the centenarian has accumulated over the centuries and which constitutes the main advantage of prolonged life. The centenarian praises from this point of view the Rosicrucians' search for the vital fluid: "Don't you see, storing up knowledge, not losing anything from individual discoveries, pursuing all power, roaming over the entire globe, knowing it in its minute details, becoming the archive of nature and humanity, . . . such a man replaces *destiny,* he is almost *God!*" (IV, 77–78). Such was the centenarian's dream, and such too was Balzac's own dream, for *La Comédie humaine* was intended as an archive of humanity, comprising in Balzac's words, "the history and criticism of society, the analysis of its ills and the discussion of its principles" (I, 20).

Another work, "L'Elixir de longue vie" ("The Elixir of Long Life"), deals with resuscitation. The owner of the elixir instructs his son in its application after the former's death. The son, however, interrupts the application so as to save the elixir for his own resuscitation *post mortem*. At the fatal moment, that man's own son, more dutiful than himself, begins faithfully to apply the elixir, but becoming frightened after anointing one arm and the head of his father, drops the vial and spills the remaining elixir. In a grotesque ending typical of the taste of the age, the cadaver, with a living arm and head, is displayed in the local cathedral as a miracle.

The works mentioned so far, however, pale into insignificance when compared with the best-known of Balzac's tales dealing with the themes of aging and death, namely *La Peau de chagrin* (variously translated as *The Wild Ass's Skin, The Onager's Skin* or *The Magic Skin*). Like *Le Centenaire, La Peau de chagrin* consists of a fantastic element within a contemporary décor, which by this stage of Balzac's development (1831) has become more realistic, with detailed and vivid descriptions and a polished narrative. The protagonist, Raphaël de Valentin, having gambled away the last bit of money remaining to him, and having been unsuccessful in winning the love of a beautiful femme fatale, Foedora, determines to commit suicide. Before doing so, however, he chances upon an antique store and enters. The owner, a man of about 125 years of age and of great wisdom and experience (like the centenarian of the earlier novel), offers Raphaël a talisman, a wild ass's skin inscribed with mysterious Sanskrit writing, which by happenstance Raphaël is able to decipher: "If you possess me, you will have everything. But your life will belong to me. God has willed it so. Wish and your wishes will be fulfilled. But measure your wishes according to your life. Here is your life: for each wish I shall shrink as the number of your days" (X,84). During the course of their conversation, the old antiquarian confides to Raphaël a great secret: "Man exhausts himself by two instinctive acts which dry up the wellsprings of his existence" (X,85). These two acts are willing and exercising one's will. The former consumes us and the latter destroys us. But there is a third alternative which the antiquarian has used to reach his advanced age: "Knowing leaves our feeble organism in a perpetual state of calm" (X,85). Having already resolved to commit suicide, and moreover skeptical of the talisman's power and the old man's sermonizing, Raphaël defiantly seizes the piece of skin and wishes for a life of riotous excess, beginning with an orgy to end all orgies. The pact is thus sealed, but nothing happens immediately, for the wishes granted by the talisman will always seem to arrive naturally. And indeed, upon leaving the shop, Raphaël encounters three friends who invite him to a fabulous party being given by a rich acquaintance. During the party, which corresponds in every respect to Raphaël's wish, the new owner of the talisman, having eaten and drunk to excess, relates his story, including his frustrations with Foedora, to a close friend. During the course of his narration, Raphaël wishes that he were rich. The next morning he learns that he has inherited a fortune from a long-lost uncle who has died in Calcutta. Taking the talisman from his pocket, Raphaël notices that it has shrunk and he is immediately seized by cold fear, for he is staring death in the face. Henceforth he will expend every effort to circumvent the force of the talisman, but to no avail. He dies at the end of the novel after formulating a final desire in spite of himself.

How are we to approach such a tale, faced with the disconcerting incongruence between the fantastic and the realistic?

From an allegorical point of view the reader can readily grasp the annunciatory function of the opening scene of the novel, which takes place in a gambling den, as well as Raphaël's subsequent visit to the antique store. Raphaël's way into the gambling den is momentarily barred by an old man crouching in the shadows who wants to check his hat. The narrator asks rhetorically whether some infernal pact is involved. The old man's face reflects a life of dissolution; in his eyes a philosopher would discern the misery of the hospital, the wanderings of bankrupts, the police reports of drowning victims, life at hard labor and exile. The old man is the traditional guardian of the gate, a Cerberus, a living warning to those who would enter. Inside, the onlookers, silent and motionless, await the strokes of fate in a bare, worn room, like spectators at a beheading. Raphaël's entrance into the gambling den is an initiation into a different world, a place of destiny, of decomposition, of death.

This passage into a world beyond prepares the identical movement into the antique shop, filled with an astonishing variety of bric-a-brac from all eras and all countries (reminiscent of the centenarian's lair). "Every country of the world seemed to have deposited there some debris from its learning, some sample of its art. It was a kind of philosophical compost heap in which nothing was lacking" (X,69). This is where Raphaël will find his destiny written on the talisman: henceforth, his suicide is merely "postponed," in the words of the antiquarian (X,88).

In this powerful allegory of the human condition, Raphaël slowly discovers the implications of the talisman's inscription. He soon realizes that the choice facing him is similar to that of Achilles in the *Iliad* (book X, lines 410–416), whose destiny was to live a short but glorious life by choosing to go to Troy, or to enjoy a long but inglorious life by choosing to stay home. Raphaël's friend sums up the situation as follows: "We can still our feelings and live a long time, or by accepting the martyrdom of passion we can die young; such is our fate" (X,118). Raphaël does what he can to evade or nullify the effect of the talisman. He cloisters himself in a mansion surrounded by servants who anticipate his every desire, he consults eminent scientists, engineers, and medical experts. He throws the talisman into a pit, but a well-meaning gardener brings it back; he even escapes from the city's corrosive temptations to live a simple life among the peasants of the Auvergne region. And finally, in a scene reminiscent of the myth of Endymion, Raphaël spends most of his time in opium-induced sleep. Each attempt fails, turning Raphaël's name ("God has healed") into a cruel joke.

La Peau de chagrin presents the human condition in the form of a dilemma: husband one's vital force by reducing the number of one's desires and live a relatively long life, or indulge one's desires and die young. Balzac's subsequent writings include characters representative of both horns of the dilemma. The usurer Gobseck, in the story of the same name, has the same gaunt figure, thin lips, pale complexion and laugh as the centenarian and the old antique dealer, and his warehouses also are filled with goods from all over the world. Like his fictional predecessors he conserves his "vital movement" (II,965), with the result that he can say: "I possess the world without fatigue; and the world has no hold on me" (II,970).

Characters representing the opposite tendency occur more often in Balzac's fiction. The courtisans in *La Peau de chagrin,* for example, are perfectly aware of their choice: "We live more in one day than a middle-class housewife in ten years" (X,116). Louis Lambert, in the short novel of that name, possesses an unusually powerful mind, but in his case the result is madness, followed by death at the age of twenty-eight. The best-known character of this group, Goriot of *Le Père Goriot (Old Man Goriot),* ruins his health because of his obsessive love for his daughters. A curious aspect of this novel is the parallelism between Goriot's financial and physical states. At the beginning of the novel Goriot has reserved for himself a comfortable retirement and his health is still good. As he nears penury because of the continual financial demands of his married daughters, Goriot's health worsens rapidly. When finally his money has completely run out, Goriot dies. Balzac has consciously or unconsciously repeated the pattern of *La Peau de chagrin,* with money as the modern counterpart of the magic talisman.

Balzac's views on the aging process underwent some changes during his lifetime. The relatively immature conception of the centenarian who has conquered time and death gives way to a maturer vision of the human condition in the allegorical magic talisman of Raphaël de Valentin. In later works, such as *Le Père Goriot, La Cousine Bette* and others, Balzac is content to depict in objective fashion the ravages of thought upon the human organism. This pessimistic portrayal of the human condition is mitigated somewhat by an article of faith which flows from Balzac's vitalist point of view. In the words of Raphaël de Valentin, who like Louis Lambert is writing an essay on the will, "the will is a material force similar to steam" (X,149). If the will, thoughts and other mental contents are material, then the question of the durability of ideas arises: "Don't ideas have a more lasting life than the body?" asks an elderly medical acquaintance of Dr. Physidor in "Les Martyrs ignorés" (XIII,742). In order to learn the implications in this for human conduct, we must turn back to the old antiquarian, who has climbed the highest mountains of Asia and America, learned all languages, lent money to a Chinese, taking his father's corpse as collateral, slept in an Arab's tent with only his word as security, and left his gold unattended in savages' wigwams:

> To know, young man, isn't that to enjoy things intuitively? Isn't it to discover the very substance of a fact and to grasp its essence? What remains of a material possession? An idea. Just think how beautiful must be the life of a man who, able to stamp all realities upon his thought, carries within his own soul the wellsprings of happiness, and then extracts from it a thousand ideal pleasures stripped of terrestrial stains. . . . What men call sorrow, love, ambition, reversal of fortune, sadness are for me ideas which I transform into dreams; instead of feeling them I express and transpose them, I develop them, I amuse myself with them like a novel which I read through an interior vision (X,86).

Although knowing in the sense of contemplation allows one to reduce the corrosive activity of thought to a minimum and thus prolong one's life to a certain degree, Balzac clearly believed (such is the lesson of *La Peau de chagrin*) that the human life span is limited. But the antiquarian's dream, which was also Balzac's dream, as well as the dream of many artists after him, points the way to a type of immortality on earth open to the creative artist alone: the work of art. Balzac's dreams are immortal, and through them so too is Balzac, for they remain crystallized for all time in the pages of *La Comédie humaine*.

6

FARCE AND IDEALIZATION: DOSTOEVSKY'S AMBIVALENCE TOWARD AGING

By Laurence M. Porter

*[*The Brothers Karamazov, *the last work of this great novelist, depicts the aging father Fyodor ruthlessly from the son's point of view. The word "senseless" is repeated four times in one description of Fyodor, and he is called by the narrator "an ill-natured buffoon and nothing more." He is a "worthless, puny weakling,* as we all called him" *(emphasis added). The narrator seems like a bitter child of this father, a solidary brother of the brothers Karamazov. The quasi-familial relationship, or at least identification, of the narrator is evident not only in the title of the work, but also in the chapter titles and in the narrative. Chapter II of the first Book is titled, for example, "He gets rid of his eldest son." And the narrator remarks that "You can easily imagine what a father such a man could be and how he could bring up his children." In this community of men and boys where sisters and mothers are absent, our story-teller is more than a mere member of the neighborhood, and at the same time less than an omniscient narrator. He is* almost *omniscient in the way that one's very close relative is. He has heard many stories; he is intimately familiar with the household, the community, and that other all-male establishment, the monastery; and he is either aware of, or able to make an educated guess about, the innermost thoughts of the characters. The tone of all*

this is that of an insider. "Why Ivan Fyodorovitch had come amongst us *I remember asking myself at the time with a certain uneasiness . . . It seemed strange on the face of it that a young man so learned, so proud, and apparently so cautious, should suddenly visit* such an infamous house and a father who had ignored him all his life. . . . " (emphasis added).

Ambivalence toward older men springs directly from ambivalence toward the father, which is vehemently demonstrated in the dichotomy between the portrayals of Fyodor, the biological father, and Zossima, the spiritual one. Zossima is devout without being stern, lighthearted without being frivolous, and a joy to be with. He is, in short, the kind of old man who is so good at putting people at ease that they unfairly decide that he is not a man at all, but a saint. Yet it is always quite clear to the reader that Zossima is truly human (although unusually insightful and good).

> *It is said that so many people had for years past come to confess their sins to Father Zossima and to entreat him for words of advice and healing, that he had acquired the keenest intuition and could tell from an unknown face what a new-comer wanted, and what was the suffering on his conscience.*

This hearsay is substantiated when Father Zossima meets Ivan and divines from one look at him the suffering which he will have to endure. The Elder, moreover, heals the sick on a routine basis. But this ability to perform "miracles" is explained by the narrator as a psychological effect. Although holy and wise, the Father is not portrayed as a saint, but as a man whose goodness makes some believe that he is one, makes most love him, and makes many envy him secretly.

The striking contrast between Fyodor and Zossima is made most dramatic when the two meet. Fyodor makes a fool of himself in a dreadful, hilarious scene, throughout which the monk treats him with firmness and kindness. Immediately thereafter, Zossima, exhausted, talks about dying soon. It is almost as if the ludicrous and evil father had sapped the strength of the benign and endearing one. Interestingly, both men are prematurely aged, Fyodor through dissipation (and for psychological and textual reasons explained by Professor Porter), and Zos-

sima possibly through the strain of empathizing with and blessing the hordes of sinners who flocked to him daily (in contemporary parlance, he's burned out). Zossima "was a short, bent, little man, with very weak legs, and although he was only sixty-five, he looked at least ten years older." For Fyodor's part, he was found several years after his wife's death to be "looking terribly aged, although he was by no means an old man. He behaved not exactly with more dignity but with more effrontery." That both should age early and be killed off in the novel shows the son's need to usurp the father, be he evil or holy.—Eds.]

AGING PREOCCUPIED DOSTOESVKY throughout his career. Old people are prominent secondary characters in four of his six major novels.[1] They are seen mainly from the viewpoint of the younger generation. This is not surprising: the characteristic literary genre of the older generation is the essay, which examines opposing opinions with detached tolerance rather than dramatizing them through conflicts between literary characters. In the moral realm, late maturity replaces the judgmental with the perceptual.

In contrast, the young person's portrayal of parental figures in the novel often reflects the pressure of emotional needs. Either these figures are idealized, expressing a child's yearning for affection and guidance, or else the child makes them farcical in an attempt to achieve the emotional distance needed to break away and achieve autonomy. Villains—the disappointing parent, object of the child's indignation—are themselves ultimately farcical: they rigidly persevere in anti-social schemes and blindly refuse to reform even in their own best interests, thus illustrating the Bergsonian comic principle of mechanical behavior imposed upon a living being. In the polarizing worlds of fiction, either comic or idealized parental figures may relate to the child through rivalry, nurture, or both. Competition may be stimulating, its absence enervating.

The extreme of rivalry is the conflict between parent and child over the same love object. Dostoevsky frequently depicts this situation. Freud's pioneering essay "Dostoevsky and Parricide" stresses the rivalry between father and son for the attentions of the mother. But when Dostoevsky eliminates the biological mother from his fiction or substitutes another object for her, the rivalry between father and son becomes even more intense. It can be displayed more overtly when suggestions of incest have been concealed by such displacement. Given this safeguard, the son's anger can be allowed to overwhelm obedience, and the father's lust to overwhelm nurturance. Old Karamazov's desire to compete with his son for the sexual favors of the alluring Grushenka betrays a failure of generativity: he tries to use his son Dmitry's inheritance to seduce Dmitry's woman. But father-daughter relationships and their multifarious disguised versions reflected in Dostoevsky's notorious (fictional) pedophilia illustrate the problems of aging in his works even more often than does rivalry between father and son.

In the perspective of intergenerational sexual conflict, fictional descriptions of old age can serve both the farcical and the idealizing aims of the implied author (the personality which can be inferred from the work as a whole) as child. To describe a man as senile or decrepit is to condemn in advance his sexual interest in younger women as inappropriate, even ludicrous. On the other hand, if he betrays no such interest, descriptions of his physical frailty add to the image of the asexual "good" father, altruistically nurturing his children and ready to give way to them in the succession of the generations.

The extreme development of nurturance in Dostoevsky appears in teacher-disciple relationships. The rigid structures of discipleship create intellectual intimacy while preserving emotional distance. In the framework of religious training, intergenerational competition is discredited and repressed: the goal is to renounce selfish desires which could be fulfilled only at the expense of others. Dostoevsky began depicting such relationships only in his late middle age: he started by presenting old age as farce.

In Dostoevsky's first literary success, the novelette *Poor People* (1847), the protagonist creates a fallacious image of his old age as a defense against a still active sexuality, revealed in his strong attraction to a much younger woman. In the saccharine opening letter, Devushkin, a self-styled "old man," complains that his vision has faded and that his eyes water. He protests that it would ill become him, at his age, to write poems as the young Barbara requests. His interest in her is purely benevolent and asexual, he claims: "A man of my advanced years, with only a tuft of hair on his head [a common castration symbol in Dostoevsky], should not let himself be involved in love affairs . . . Poor orphan that you are, I regard myself simply as your father" (pp. 2–11). The disclaimer is unconvincing, and we learn that he is only forty-six or seven. To nearly every one in his boarding house, Devushkin is a comic, infatuated figure. He makes drastic financial sacrifices to buy Barbara frivolous presents. At length, penury obliges her to accept a marriage of convenience with a rich, odious suitor. Only as she departs do she and Devuskin helplessly avow their pathetic mutual love. The story's title *Poor People* is a red herring. The author abets his protagonist's ego-defense by using realistic descriptions of poverty to keep the lovers apart. Thus he preserves the incest taboo which Devushkin's delusions of old age are by themselves inadequate to preserve.

Soon after this publication Dostoevsky's career was interrupted for nearly ten years by prison and then involuntary military service in Siberia. Shortly after his release he published the novelette *Uncle's Dream* (1859). He admitted it was "tossed off in haste," adding that old Prince K. is "the only serious figure in the whole tale."[2] This Prince is a decrepit, loquacious person too senile even to recognize old acquaintances (pp. 230–31). He has false teeth, a wig, a leg of cork and a glass eye—but he still admires pretty women and spends much of each day primping. His heirs are trying to have him committed to an asylum so that he will not remarry and leave his fortune to a new wife. When Prince K. visits a provincial town, its scheming social leader tries to trick him into proposing to her daughter. He seems disoriented enough to be completely malleable. Zina, the proud and beautiful daughter, is bullied into singing for him. His delighted praise is willfully misconstrued by the mother as a proposal. But in a moment of unaccustomed boldness, Zina's silly young suitor frightens Prince K. out of the marriage and convinces the befuddled old man that his "proposal" was merely a dream.

Had the novelette ended this way Prince K. would have been nothing more than a traditional comic figure like the old men in folkdances who become excited during a carnival, rise to join the dancers, and gyrate grotesquely for a few moments before falling back aching and exhausted. But a comic epilogue tells that Zina has moved to another town after her mother's public humiliation, and married a general—a symbolic father-figure. This undermines her previous status as a romantic, star-crossed heroine whose true love had killed himself. The old man's feelings prove more profound than hers. He dies of a "moral shock" a few days after retracting his proposal. In retrospect, we understand that his mental confusion and helplessness do not mean that he cannot have an intense emotional life. And although his sexuality has been presented as comical, neither he nor the author attempts to conceal it as had been done in *Poor People* twelve years before.

Two years later, Dostoevsky's first full-length novel, *The Insulted and the Injured* (1861), presents the father's fixation on the daughter more directly still. No longer do surrogate daughters pursue father-figures: real daughters leave their old fathers to follow seducers. These fathers, unable to forgive their daughters, indulge themselves in "the egoism of suffering" (p. 273). For their children to cease to be children is an unpardonable sin. Generativity has been thwarted by possessiveness. This is a middle-aged person's problem. Dostoevsky disguises it as an old person's problem here since biological daughters rather than surrogate daughters are involved. He must desexualize the fathers to ward off a threat of incest more immediate than before.[3]

There are two possessive fathers in the novel: the foreigner Smith, whom the narrator does not know, and the family friend Ichmenyev, whose daughter the narrator loves. Smith's existence is mysterious. Only in flashbacks does he speak coherently; in the present time of narration his mumbled words are enigmatic. These alien qualities associate him with the unconscious, which we can perceive only vaguely. Such distancing makes it possible for the narrator's relationship with Smith to illustrate the latent Oedipal motifs of symbolic murder and displacement without the narrator's guilt becoming too strong.

The narrator has an unpleasant presentiment when he sees Smith on the street at the beginning of the novel. Soon after, he witnesses the death of the old man's dog in a café, and the old man's death outside. The narrator symbolically displaces the surrogate father, Smith, by moving into his wretched room and becoming the protector of Smith's granddaughter Nelly, who falls in love with him. The narrator's fears that the old man's ghost may appear reveal some guilt, but he feels justified in displacing Smith because the old man, unbending and tyrannical, broke off relations with his daughter when she eloped; and he remained withdrawn even after she became destitute.

What the narrator takes from one father-figure he must sacrifice to another. This other is Nikolay Sergevitch Ichmenyev, a former estate steward whose daughter left him to have an affair with his employer's son. Ichmenyev loves his daughter so intensely that he weeps secretly in her absence, but he will not forgive her for leaving him. He plans to replace her by taking in the little orphan girl, Nelly, to keep him company. The narrator relinquishes her as he had relinquished his claims to Ichmenyev's daughter, and Nelly becomes the instrument of Ichmenyev's redemption. She promptly understands the similarities between his situation and her own grandfather's (Part II, chapter ix, pp. 157–158): "He's wicked . . . He won't forgive his daughter." She later berates Ichmenyev for this (Part IV, chapter iv). Finally, by telling the story of how her own mother died before her repentant grandfather could reach her, she provokes Nikolay's wife Anna to set forth in search of her daughter. Anna's initiative breaks through Ichmenyev's reserve and allows him to act upon his repressed love for his missing child (Part IV, chapter vii). They are reconciled. Nelly immediately has an epileptic fit and soon afterwards dies, loving and beloved by everyone. Her passionate, spontaneous affection has pointed up by contrast the old men's fault of cutting themselves off from love in the present by clinging to the past.

On a deeper level, the narrator defends himself against feelings of Oedipal rivalry by replacing his own father with Ichmenyev and then replacing Ichmenyev with Smith. Unresolved emotional problems often generate such chains of symbolic substitutions.[4] Smith as "bad father" becomes a permissible target for the narrator's aggressive feelings aroused by his own courtship of Ichmenyev's daughter. It is as if the narrator were imagining "What if I won that daughter? Then I would [symbolically] kill Ichmenyev by supplanting him, and he would take vengeance [by returning as a ghost, as guilt]." The narrator acts out this fantasy in a displaced, desexualized form with Smith's granddaughter. Latent pedophilia serves as a defense against the dangers of sexual rivalry with the father-figure. It is as if the narrator fantasized that "If I take a pre-pubescent girl, I am not taking anything the father wants; if sexual performance with that girl is not at issue, I do not need to measure myself against the sexual performance of the father, who has already procreated successfully; I need more time to develop my self-esteem; besides, his own daughter is always available to him anyway." In the intitial scene, the exaggerated depiction of Smith's old age (his daughter must be only in her early thirties), poverty, senility and helplessness remove him from effective competition with the narrator. He is a safe opponent. At the same time the narrator "undoes" any possibility of rivalry with the other symbolic father, Ichmenyev: he gives up Nelly to Ichmenyev as if to atone for having desired to take Ichmenyev's daughter.

Filial guilt, producing a welter of renunciation and helplessness, leaves a void at the center of the novel. The narrator Ivan Petrovich proves to be a pseudo-hero, a mere passive intermediary and errand-boy. The truly dominant figure is the potent "bad father" Prince Volkovsky. "His evil will determines the fate of all the personages." As the unjust former employer of Ichmenyev, the true father of Nelly, and the father of the childish weakling who has won Ichmenyev's daughter, he unites all the plots. Absent from the first and last of the four parts of the novel, he reveals his moral loathsomeness directly only in part three, exulting in his ability to expose himself to the narrator with impunity. But in the end he totally triumphs: he prevents his son Alyosha's marriage to the impecunious Natasha and himself prepares to marry a wealthy fourteen-year-old girl.[5] Thematically the novel condemns him; mimetically he reigns supreme.

Although his son Alyosha is no younger than Ichmenyev's daughter Natasha, Volkovsky in contrast to Ichmenyev is portrayed in vigorous middle age. His noble rank of Prince enhances his paternal status. The way he takes over the novel reveals that all the implied author's defenses against rivalry with the father have broken down: compliance (Ivan Petrovich's acts of renunciation), aggression (describing Ichmenyev and Smith as old and helpless), and withdrawal (removing Volkovsky from the scene at the beginning and ending of the work). A similar subversion of filial strategies will recur in *A Raw Youth* where the vigorous middle-aged father Versilov ultimately steals the scenes.

Dostoevsky's next novel, *Crime and Punishment* (1864), experiments with particularly violent forms of reaction against parental figures. The unworthy symbolic father Marmeladov is reduplicated by immoral middle-aged suitors of the hero's sister (Luzhin and Svidrigailov), and complemented by the phallic mother Alyena Ivanova, the pawnbroker, while the biological father is absent. Not all the violence in the novel has been recognized for what it is: an explosion of filial rebellion.

The novel begins when the hero Raskolnikov learns that his sister intends to marry the pompous, self-centered Luzhin, sacrificing herself in order to obtain funds to maintain him at the university. He urgently desires to find money to prevent this. The only source of money he knows about is the wealthy old pawnbroker who already holds several of his heirlooms in pawn. Then in a tavern he overhears a debate between a student (symbolic son) and an officer (symbolic father). The former, articulating Raskolnikov's own thoughts, claims it is justifiable to kill the pawnbroker provided that you use her idle money for the good of humanity.

> On the one hand you have a stupid, silly, utterly unimportant, vicious, sickly old woman, no good to anybody . . . On the other hand . . . a hundred, a thousand, good actions and promising beginnings might be forwarded and directed aright by the money that old woman destines for a monastery . . . What is the life of that stupid, spiteful, consumptive old woman weighed against the common good? (p.62).

The string of insults and the incoherent exaggeration of the numbers renders the utilitarian argument suspect; and the officer scornfully tells the student that since he actually intends to do nothing, his arguments are pointless. Raskolnikov takes up the challenge by killing the pawnbroker, but his resolve to help others remains theoretical. Without even counting the stolen money, he hides it under a great stone. To cover his tracks after the murder he kills Alyena's younger sister Lizaveta, the one person the old woman had most oppressed—and her unborn child. One recalls Ivan's question to Alyosha in *The Brothers Karamazov:* would you consent to found universal happiness on the suffering and death of one innocent child? Do those too young or too old to contribute to society deserve to live when others might benefit from their death? May any life be taken for the good of all?[6]

Raskolnikov says yes, but he also feels the need to justify his crime on esthetic grounds, by stressing the old woman's ugliness, pettiness, and meanness. Eliminating her makes the world look more attractive. This argument, however, works against other elements of Raskolnikov's self-justification. The slaying of a feeble old woman has little in common with the heroic military feats of the Napoleon whom Raskolnikov fancies as a model of the amoral superman. And it is paradoxical that our self-styled nihilist feels more justified in killing an old person than a younger one. In fact Raskolnikov's childish resentment and need for exoneration lead him to exaggerate Alyena's physical decrepitude. She is described as if she were in her seventies, but her sister is pregnant—she couldn't be much older than fifty-five.[7] The fascinated horror with which Raskolnikov studies her physical appearance seems to derive from his own fear of aging. He particularly fears to age without having realized his idealized self-image. A dread of failure prevents him from acting. Throughout the work he seems paralyzed by anxiety about putting himself to the test. He avoids possibilities for remunerative employment which would allow him to continue at the university; he remains nearly immobile in his room for days at a time.

The artificial agedness of the pawnbroker embodies the narcissistic self's fears of being threatened by passing time. The opposite extreme of oblivious self-absorption appears in the unnatural, subtly evil youthfulness of the middle-aged Svidrigailov and Luzhin. Their physical appearance is coquettishly well-preserved. Both are sexually interested in Raskolnikov's sister, and both are severely punished by the implied author for this attempted generational transgression. Luzhin is publicly humiliated and disgraced; Svidrigailov goes insane and shoots himself. In the same world, these displaced forms of the obsessive father-son-daughter triangle find a much more melodramatic echo where the symbolic son's rage and resulting desire for self-punishment are fully, although indirectly, revealed.

By chance, Raskolnikov meets an alcoholic ex-clerk, Marmeladov, and hears his confession. Marmeladov spends all his family's meager funds on drink; his daughter Sonia has become a prostitute to try to support them; thus the father is abusing his daughter's sexuality. Not long afterwards, Raskolnikov again runs into Marmeladov when the latter, dead drunk, is trampled by a team of horses. Raskolnikov gets Marmeladov to his own bed, but his chest has been crushed and he soon dies. Sonia and Raskolnikov are brought together by this death of the unworthy father. When he later admits to her that he has murdered the pawnbroker, she insists that he surrender to the police; after his trial and sentencing she follows him to Siberia; eventually he is converted there. Both the initially comic drunkenness and the episodic appearance of Maremladov conceal the symbolic seriousness of his wish-fulfilling death. It restores the victimized daughter's purity but necessitates the expiation of the son-surrogate's guilt before he can be united with her.

Like the pawnbroker's hoarding, Marmeladov's spendthriftiness represents a parental failure to nurture. Either extreme excites the rage of the child, which the implied author mediates through descriptions of old age and drunkenness. At a deeper level, Raskolnikov feels anger at his biological mother because her poverty makes it impossible for her to provide for him. By pawning family heirlooms, he symbolically severs his connection with his disappointing family. The pawnbroker, by "unjustly" withholding these heirlooms at extortionate rates of interest, becomes an admissible target for redirected, inadmissible anger.

While Dostoevsky composed his following short novel, *The Gambler* (1866), he was falling in love with his secretary, a woman twenty-five years younger than he. Perhaps as a result, he depicts old age as superficially farcical (the outsider's initial, unreflective attitude toward his situation) but fundamentally admirable (latent self-justification). He portrays an apparently dotty, doddering aunt of seventy-five. Hearing that she has fallen seriously ill, her impoverished nephew inquires feverishly whether she has yet died, in frequent communications to her home town. He wants her money to buy the love of a demi-mondaine. But she recovers sufficiently to journey to the spa where her nephew is awaiting her death. She confronts and discomfits him and gambles away most of her fortune in his presence. But first impressions are misleading. She is lucid, not senile. When she discovers roulette for the first time she becomes obsessed with it, but she, unlike the eponymic young tutor, at length frees herself from the game and learns a lesson: "Henceforward I won't blame young people for being flighty" (p. 93). She is not a rigid, limited character. Gambling suggests self-absorption; by renouncing it, the old aunt proves to be the only generative person in the story, generously providing at last for her foolish nephew's two youngest, neglected children.

Two major novels—*The Idiot* and *The Possessed*—intervened before Dostoevsky again took up the problem of aging. Dostoevsky was entering late middle age when the novel *A Raw Youth* appeared in 1875. He was a year older than several fifty-five-year-old male characters whom he describes as "old": Bishop Tihon, the writer Karmazinov in *The Possessed,* and the father of *The Brothers Karamazov. A Raw Youth* reflects a transition in Dostoevsky's self-concept and therefore betrays a confusion of viewpoints. The twenty-year-old bastard Dolgurky narrates it; his father Versilov, in his middle forties, gradually takes over and dominates the action; Dolgurky's nominal father Makar Ivanovitch, who is seventy, represents spiritual wisdom. He illustrates an ideal of ecstatic religious experience and forgiveness, but exerts little practical influence upon events: it seems that Dostoevsky has come to believe that old people can provide valuable guidance but that he has not yet integrated this belief into the structure of his novels.

A Raw Youth tells the reconciliation of Dolgurky with the father who neglected him for twenty years. Despite not having lived with his son, Versilov displays preternatural insight regarding his feelings and innermost thoughts. Thus this father-figure becomes partially fused with the omniscient author concealed behind the screen of the son's narration. But Versilov, who belongs to the middle generation, never pronounces in one way or the other on the meaning and value of old age.

Dolgurky, the adolescent narrator, begins with an awkward, stilted, self-conscious style. His naïveté makes him feel mingled scorn and awe toward old age, while the artificiality of his style allows the implied author subtly to dissociate himself from either of these extreme viewpoints. Dolgurky has three decisive encounters with old people. First he works as companion and private secretary for the senile, kindly Prince Sokulsky; then he meets the saintly Makar, who is dying; finally he ineffectually shelters the Prince from relatives angered at the prospect of his remarriage.

Old Prince Sokolsky—actually, he is only sixty—has had a nervous breakdown a year and a half before the novel begins. He resigned from the service and thenceforth at times displayed "an excessive frivolity . . . not quite appropriate to his years, [and] of which . . . there was no sign in him before . . . [Allegedly, he] developed a marked disposition to rush into matrimony" (p. 20). Therefore his heirs, alarmed at the prospect of dividing their birthright with a stepmother, guard him carefully. A widower for the past twenty years, the Prince has been sublimating his desire to remarry. He takes poor female relatives into his household while they are still children, has them well educated, finds them husbands, and provides them with a dowry. Since his fit, he fears others may consider him mad. To prove that his mind has remained sound, he often makes speeches and sprinkles his conversation with "profound reflections and *bons mots*" (p. 20). His wisdom, however, is conventional, and serves as a counterphobic display of verbal mastery.

To characterize Prince Sokolsky, Dolgurky uses the cliché that old age is a second childhood. Sokolsky treats his secretary with childlike simplicity. "If he had been put into our school and in the fourth class too [among fifteen-year-olds], what a nice school-fellow he would have made." But since his attack, his expression would change disconcertingly and without warning from "excessive gravity" to "exaggerated playfulness." This lack of emotional consistency is reflected in his fascination with two subjects at opposite extremes of profundity: speculation concerning the existence of God, and gossip about women (p. 24). Dolgurky is troubled by the old Prince's lack of emotional self-control because it reminds him uncomfortably of his own. He also feels humiliated at the suspicion that he may be a mere paid companion rather than a secretary with legitimate work to do. He frequently absents himself for considerable periods in order to demonstrate to himself his independence.

Eager to mature, Dolgurky frankly avows and condemns his social awkwardness and inexperience (pp. 242, 293, 444). The raw youth serves as a barometer by which the greater maturity of old age can be measured. But in this novel Dostoevsky does not equate aging with the automatic achievement of emotional and spiritual maturity: to do so would eliminate free choice and free will from his vision of human beings. Instead, he depicts two courses which human development in old age may follow: becoming tranquilly at one with the universe, or becoming like a frightened child.

The stresses of Dolgurky's quest for independence bring on an attack of "brain fever"—an illness which, together with the unexpected, revelatory letter, is the favorite *Deus ex machina* of the nineteenth-century novel. Crushed by self-loathing, he needs a new father-figure to guide him. A few days after regaining consciousness—an event he describes as "my resurrection" (p. 346)—Dolgurky finds himself alone in bed and intensely irritable. Suddenly he hears a voice saying "Lord Jesus Christ, have mercy upon us." He seeks the speaker and finds an ailing but strongly-built man with a broad white beard. He guesses that this is his mother's legal husband Makar Ivanovitch Dolgurky, the serf whom he has never seen before. Delighted that his stepson is now well enough to leave his bed, the old man laughs for joy, in a "childlike and incredibly attractive" reaction. "You are young, it is good for you," he says. "The old monk looks toward the grave, but the young must live." Although Makar has loved life, he faces death "with blissful resignation" (pp. 350–351). When Dolgurky disagrees with him about religion in their ensuing conversations, he does not become impatient or angry: he speaks with unvarying affection and selfless concern. The youth is drawn to Makar's "seemliness" (lack of sexual, material, and egotistical interests), which offers a reassuring lack of competition and contrasts with the character of others whom he knows. He is touched by Makar's "large-hearted generosity" in forgiving his wife for leaving him. Impulsively he plans to follow Makar on his pilgrimages, for he longs for a role-model who will aid him in suppressing his own embarrassing desires. "I won't follow them, I don't know where I'm going, I'll go with you" (p. 356).

Unexpectedly, Dolgurky's interest in Makar advances his reconciliation with his real father, Versilov. Dolgurky discovers with surprise that Versilov cares about Makar for his own sake, and not merely because of the old man's connection to Versilov's mistress. "I must confess if it had not been for Versilov I should have overlooked and failed to appreciate a great deal in this old man" (p. 377). Makar continues his friendly arguments with his stepson, defending the values of prayer and of withdrawal from the temptations of the world against Dolgurky's ideal of actively serving mankind. Without renouncing his own opinions, Dolgurky comes to recognize how greatly the old man could be a source of solace and guidance for others. His serenity offers a corrective to the hectic search for happiness on the part of many of the other characters.

Shortly after Makar dies, old Prince Sokolsky reappears in the story. His daughter, Katarina Nikolaevna, threatens to send him to a madhouse because he intends to marry Dolgurky's legitimate half-sister. He feels helpless and needs protection as well as companionship. "Since I had seen him last," Dolgurky observes, "they had turned the old man, till lately almost hale, and to some extent rational, and not altogether without will-power, into a sort of mummy, a scared and mistrustful child" (p. 521). He takes refuge in Dolgurky's flat; the latter, now able to dominate the relationship, feels compassion rather than the embarrassment, amusement, and irritation he had felt before. After a scandalous scene there, the fiancé of the Prince's daughter takes him home. But he is reconciled with his daughter, who relents. The Prince regains his lucidity and dies quietly a month later. But this episode has briefly reversed Dolgurky's and Prince Sokolsky's respective roles of dependent and protector. The former thus acquires a new sense of autonomy. The novel ends on several notes of promise for the future, concluding with the words "from raw youths are made up the generations." Although the old men die in the novel, their interaction with the younger generations has prepared a constructive continuation of society.

In Dostoevsky's final novel, *The Brothers Karamazov* (1881), the old monk Zossima's exemplary account of his life is a modified version of traditional Russian Orthodox hagiography.[8] But it has more weight than the story of a saint's life because it is presented in Zossima's own words—or more accurately, in Alyosha's synthesis of what he remembers of Zossima's words. The account of Zossima's conversion answers, in a way which Christ's life cannot, the ordinary person's question concerning how to move from sin to sanctity.

Zossima's salient quality is his keen intuition of the spiritual sufferings of those who come from far and wide to consult him. This gift derives from years of pastoral experience with penitents and pilgrims (p. 26). Zossima surpasses his prototype, Makar, in his understanding of human nature as he does in his sense of his teaching mission. For the monk "is responsible to all men . . . This knowledge is the crown of life for the monk and for every man." Therefore, before he died Zossima was eager "to say everything he had not said in his life . . . as though thirsting to share with all men and all creation his joy and ecstasy" (p. 177). He is a model of Eriksonian integrity and solidarity.

As Zossima himself explains, tolerance, forgiveness, and renunciation result naturally during the life cycle, whereby "the mild serenity of age takes the place of the riotous blood of youth" (p. 322). This phrase is not a mere rationalization of self-effacement made inescapable by the weaknesses of age. What Zossima actually does in interpersonal relations shows him to be healthy. He does not let himself be dominated or exploited. He is kind and accepting of others, but does not make renunciation into a way of life.

Dostoevsky has Zossima die two-fifths of the way through the novel so that there will be ample room to depict the effects of the old man's example on his survivors. At first Alyosha hopes for miracles after Zossima's death and wants to bask in his reflected glory. He is dismayed by the rapid decay of the corpse, superstitiously considered a sign of the lack of God's favor. But during his vigil by the corpse he falls asleep and sees his old teacher in a dream. He experiences a decisive conversion. "He had fallen on the earth a weak boy, but he rose up a resolute champion" (p. 404). (Dostoevsky planned a sequel to the novel in which Alyosha would have gone into the world—as Zossima had advised him—to become a leader.) In the novel's closing phrase, "Hurrah for Karamazov!", with which a group of boys hail Alyosha's benevolent spiritual guidance, the succession of generations is affirmed. Thus with the aid of the idealized surrogate father, Zossima, Alyosha symbolically succeeds and displaces his cowardly, clownish real father, Fyodor Petrovitch, whose name is the title of the novel's opening chapter.

In conjunction with Father Zossima, old Fyodor Petrovitch Karamazov—an inveterate, prematurely aged sensualist—introduces to the novel the Oedipally-colored myth of dual parentage, of the materialistic "bad" father and the spiritualized "good" father. *A Raw Youth* already sketched this contrast by pairing Versilov with Makar Ivanovitch. The bad father either neglects his offspring, or contends with them for sex or money, or both. The immoderate insults with which Dostoevsky characterizes the elder Karamazov suggest that to the last the Oedipal stresses in his fiction were never entirely resolved. Fyodor Petrovitch is vehemently condemned from the outset as "a type abject and vicious and at the same time senseless . . . a worthless, puny weakling . . . an ill-natured buffoon . . . voluptuous," loving to humiliate himself, and inspiring revulsion in nearly everyone (pp. 1–4). His physical appearance is equally loathsome (p. 19). He sums up his life plan thus: "As I get older, you know, I shan't be a pretty object. The wenches won't come to me of their own accord, so I shall want my money" (p. 188). He functions as the lowest common denominator of sensualism. By contrast he exalts the supreme individuality of Zossima's spirituality. More directly than it is raised in *Crime and Punishment,* he raises the issue of whether non-generative parents deserve to live. All four of his sons desire his death, although in Alyosha this feeling is deeply repressed.[9] So they all feel guilty when he dies. The actual murderer among them, Smerdyakov, kills himself; Dmitri punishes himself by accepting an unjust judicial condemnation for his father's death—although he plans to remain with the woman his father had wanted; Ivan goes temporarily insane; only Alyosha escapes relatively unscathed. But he has shown himself vulnerable to temptation, and Dostoevsky carefully avoids pronouncing on the ultimate destiny of all three surviving brothers. He believes neither in fate nor in psychological determinism, but in Providence: the verdict is not yet in.

This is not to say that Dostoevsky unquestioningly endorses all spirituality. To illustrate the possible excesses of the monastic life, which can conceal jealousy and the drive toward self-glorification, he introduces the withdrawn, ascetic, devil-haunted old Father Ferapont. But his exaggerated condemnation of old Karamazov implies that old people should give up sexual activity. One recalls how old Prince Sokolsky in *A Raw Youth* remained "almost hale" until he became interested in marrying a young woman, at which point he was reduced to "a frightened child" as if he had been punished by the implied author. The social taboo against sexuality in the aged, widespread from the Middle Ages until the very recent past, persists in masked forms in Dostoevsky. In conjunction with his fantasies of pedophilia, it betrays a troubled, ambivalent attitude toward aging and sexuality.

As Dostoevsky's career progressed, his fiction took old people more and more seriously. It moved increasingly toward presenting them in their own words and having them offer constructive guidance to others. During Dostoevsky's own middle age, however, certain characters are artificially aged in order to disguise the middle-aged problem of generativity; as old people, they do not fully exist in their own right. Moreover, old people are expendable in Dostoevsky's fiction. They often die early on, once their influence no longer is needed to move the plot. In part, this state of affairs is realistic: old people do tend to die sooner than others; and it also reflects a healthy acceptance of the succession of generations. But it suggests as well a failure of identification with old people by the implied author. Dostoevsky gradually came to see that wisdom and spiritual maturity could sometimes compensate for physical deterioration. But, probably because his attitudes toward sexuality remained conflicted, he did not resolve the problem of reconciling aging with sexuality. His depictions of sexuality in the elderly are stereotyped; their choices are lust or nothing. The sexual father tends always to want to possess the daughter and to vie with the son. Dostoevsky's fiction evades the problem of sexual attraction to mothers by depicting them either as phallic or self-effacing. And in *The Brothers Karamazov* biological mothers and daughters are absent from the main family: Dostoevsky skirts the issue of relationships with them. But with the partial exception of Versilov in *A Raw Youth,* he never portrays an older male who can be wise, nurturant, and a sexual being all at once.

7

PROUSTIAN OLD AGE, OR THE KEY TO TIME RECAPTURED

By Diana Festa-McCormick

[Professor Festa-McCormick's chapter illuminates the final social event of Proust's masterpiece through an examination of images of old age in it and their effect on the narrator, Marcel. Marcel is an astute observer of his social surroundings. He notes that Mme de Guermantes has lost her wittiness, for example. "Late in life, fatigued by the least effort, Mme de Guermantes said an enormous number of idiotic things . . . " She is forgetful. She thinks, for example, that Marcel was a part of her elite circle several years earlier than he actually was. He is struck by this error, because he vividly remembers that important period of trying to enter her world. Marcel laments that passing time brings with it memory loss and thus a diminishing of the world he cherished. Newcomers and the younger generation accurately perceive their elders' faults, but they cannot appreciate simultaneously the other side: the sparkle, the wit, the elegance, and the subtlety of those Marcel remembers so vividly. As Diana Festa-McCormick demonstrates, Marcel must recapture lost time through the work of art if the richness and poignancy of the world he knew are not to be lost forever. Only through the novel will he be able to convey to others the complexity of his time and milieu. For his is a nonchalant class, rather forgetful of details of its own past—even of its dead—and the

aged have already faded almost as completely. And so Marcel resolves, at the end of the novel, to write the story of his life: the work which Proust had just finished writing and which we have just finished reading.

What Proust says of the role of memory in artistic creation can be applied to the aging person's life tasks. Erikson presented self-evaluation as a major life task. Before you die, you need to take stock, not for art's sake nor even as a form of art, but for its inherent personal value. And Robert Butler provides a methodology for achieving this task in several important statements geared toward clinical practice. One needn't be an Augustine, Montaigne, or Proust, an autobiographer, essayist, poet or painter, to experience a sense of selfhood before leaving this world. One needn't, either, have a memory perfectly intact. For the memory is selective, and those people and events which are salient to the person looking back are implicitly of greatest meaning—Eds.]

OLD AGE, like many realities found within vaguely delineated confines, can perhaps best be defined in medical terms—as a weakening of muscle responses, or circulatory impediment, or glandular malfunction. To the naked eye, it rests on subjective individual perception. For a ten-year-old his thirty-year-old mother may appear venerable, while those who will never see forty again must think differently. The perception in Proust's *Remembrance of Things Past* is of course that of the narrator, whose sense of time is so permeated with emotions as to reside almost totally outside the calendar.

As a child, the protagonist-narrator Marcel had been in awe of Parisian aristocracy. As a young man, he learned how to become socially accepted by them. After a long absence, he returns to Paris, middle-aged and weary. Hundreds of pages in the last volume of Proust's novel relate his rediscovery of this aristocracy, mainly a generation older than he, at a party given by the Duke of Guermantes. Readers do not know how many years have lapsed when Marcel meets again, at the end, all the people whose existence had seemed so important to him in the past. One may take account of the intervening war years, but those would not in themselves justify the dramatic changes he finds in everyone upon returning to Paris. How long he has been confined in a nursing home also remains unclear. Unquestionable, however, is his overwhelming shock at that sudden confrontation with passing time, after the years spent away from his circle of acquaintances. Time is visibly reduced to space through a kind of satanic masquerade that appears more like a *danse macabre* than a Parisian social event. A life span can be measured by the signs of age evident upon all faces—and envisioned like a line, all too brief, that lacks a mere dot or two before completion.

The masks that whirl at the party—unrecognizable people with parchment features and staccato movements, with only traces of the bright smiles of their youth—advance toward Marcel, threatening to upset the orderly world of his memories, the stages that brought him on wings of fantasy along gilded paths of wonderment and adulation. Here are the very people who had set him to dreaming, their feet of clay now all too visible beneath distorted bodies. Time is suddenly dislocated, shattering his past with its illusions and disappointments. The ghosts crowding the Guermantes' great hall glide by like accomplices of deeds untold to him. Their hands reach threateningly back toward his cherished images, to contaminate and reduce them.

Marcel's shock is not so much linked with old age per se as with death, with the shadow of nothingness that looms beyond all those figures. Finality abruptly intrudes as he senses for the first time his own perishability and that of his memories. Age in itself would be meaningless were it not for the tension it establishes with the past, and youth is more meaningful from the perspective of age. Old age is thus not only the last step toward death, but also a time for shaping memory and for rebirth through art. Within old age reside the potential for creation and the spark that may lead to a work of art. This essay will attempt to follow Marcel's perceptive eye as he measures the dimension of time in the perspective of his own life span, before he refutes the disruptive aspect of old age and man's mortality through a lasting and perennially vibrant work of art.

Continuity in life is maintained mostly through passive acquiescence to habits. In Proust's world, habits are composed, on the whole, of social encounters, of slipping from gown to gown or from tuxedo to tails, of walks along the avenues of the Bois, of encounters for tea or dinner, and then after dinner of a visit or two, of some ball or other. With smiles of understanding or impenetrable glares, people are acknowledged or ignored, encouraged to ascend the golden ladder to social recognition or pushed down pitilessly to oblivion. The days are thus filled, and they slip into months, years. People see and recognize each other, and if time has exacted its toll upon their features, they hardly notice it. They continue exchanging barbs or pleasantries, drawing imperceptibly closer each time to their final encounter, with only passing remarks on the absence of those who have already departed. They do not realize, Marcel suddenly understands at that last party at the Princess of Guermantes', that their destination is death. A sense of imminence seizes him, as he watches etched upon the grotesque figures around him the reflection of his own mortality.

The device used to uncover all pretense and reveal to Marcel's startled eyes what amounts to a synchronized march to waiting graves, is that of his own protracted absence from the Parisian social scene. The evidence of old age, absurdly encroaching upon the vitality of all those whom his memory retains as in the prime of their youth, is an unambiguous revelation only for him. He alone has stayed away and allowed a gap to grow between what he recalls and the stark reality of the present. "The first moment I did not understand why I hesitated to recognize the master of the house, the guests, and why they all appeared 'made up,' with powdered hair that completely changed their looks" (p. 921). Surely the people assembled there have no difficulty in recognizing each other, nor are they surprised by the lack of luster in each other's appearance. The masquerade exists only for Marcel. He is little more than an intruder into his own past, wondering why the dashing Prince of old has absurdly stuck "a white beard" to his chin.

What emerges from the carnavalesque gathering at the Prince of Guermantes' is a complex view of age, intrinsically linked with the individuals' sense of time and, like seasons, both perishable and renewable. If the central perspective is that of the narrator, secondary motifs also emerge intermittently, brought to the fore through his intuitive responses to them. They provide an accompaniment to Marcel's musings. Essentially, one may divide those varying views of old age into three categories. The first is Marcel's. The second is lived by the aged people themselves, unaware of the extent of the devastation that the passing of years has wrought upon them, and vanquished in their effort to camouflage it. The third belongs to an unconcerned younger generation, present if nameless, uncomprehending and frivolous in the face of the demands of the past. This last aspect is the least apparent, the backdrop against which the scene is played out. The young are the casual spectators of what will later become their own drama, unconscious participants in a seasonal performance. And they are a visible yardstick against which life can be measured in its quick progression. Marcel wants to apprehend the whole of a life span, retaining its discrete stages, so that youth may endure in the perspective of age, and so that duration may be extorted from his own incipient death.

The danger that confronts Marcel at the Guermantes' reception is the possibility that the spent eyes and dull complexions he now sees around him could detract from the purity and the beauty of his recollections. He cannot, as with an album, simply turn the page back, concentrate his attention there, and allow earlier pictures to stand at last side by side with the latest ones. There are no pages to turn yet, not until he enfolds all the images he carries in his mind within the book he yearns to write.

Oriane de Guermantes runs like a leitmotif through the pages of *Remembrance*. She first set Marcel to dreaming in the early Combray days, a mere name then, but one that evoked visions of glory and ineffable beauty, all perceivable in the cascades of golden light thrust upon the somber walls of his room, from the magic lantern by his bed. The young man then sees her, from afar at first, gradually closer; he is mystified, enraptured, then thrilled, and finally charmed. She has forever been for him the symbol of refinement, elegance, and glamour. She reigned unchallenged over the Parisian salons of his youth. But she now partakes of the sinister festivity before him, having been driven by the frenzied merry-go-round of time like all the others.

> I had just noticed her, walking between a double row of staring people who, without realizing the wonderful artifices of clothing and aesthetics that operated upon them, touched by that red head of hair, that salmon pink body barely emerging from its black lace fins, and choked with jewels, looked at it, within the hereditary sinuosity of its lines, as they would have done for some ancient sacred fish, laden with precious stones, in which was incarnated the guardian spirit of the Guermantes family (p. 927).

It is not merely a woman who advances between the parted rows, but the emblem of an epoch, wrapped as it were in gauze, a museum object that hermetically encapsulates the secret of its being. Its only life resides in memory, and the people around do not remember. They were not there in the days of her glory, they did not breathe the electrifying air of her live presence. This younger generation, these fresh faces unmarked yet by the passage of time, stand there both in awe and bemusement, as they would before "some ancient sacred fish, laden with precious stones." The three perspectives in the vision of age are here evident, that represented by the "staring people," of course, those who are too young to have known Oriane in her glory; by the narrator; and by Oriane herself. The Duchess has applied all her artistry in trying to camouflage the marks of age, and clings to her role, like a queen whose extended reign remains a matter of protocol but whose power has long since passed into other hands. But the vigor that once was hers is only mimicked now, much as the past sinuosity of her body is simulated beneath swathes of black lace. Surely there is no relation between this carefully preserved object and the sparkling princess of old. An immense hiatus separates them—a short stretch in the spectrum of verifiable time, yet infinite in personal duration. But duration is the stuff of dreams, and dreams are the stuff of art. "I realized for the first time," the narrator admits in bewilderment, "that the time which had gone by for them . . . had also gone by for me"

(p. 927). And when Oriane calls him "my oldest friend," all illusions are shattered about youth still tarrying in him alone amidst the shadows of his past. "Surely she exaggerates," he protests. But still, "am I then . . . " The question is left in mid-air, but its echo lingers on. It stands as a warning and a threat that can no longer be conjured away. Yes, he too must have aged, the last hour is also approaching for him, and the tender beauty of his recollections may soon be buried with him. The figures before him are nothing but the materialization of that new fear, the visible *memento mori* that started to haunt him the moment he entered the great reception hall. Those figures appear to be already engulfed in the shadow of waiting graves. There are women whose skirts are evidently entangled "on their sepulchral vault" (p. 938) and men who limp as if dragged toward a gaping void.

Marcel's mission, but a formless desire until now, gradually takes shape. And so he begins to store in his mind the Goyesque shapes that surround him—much as he had done for those of the past—no longer fighting them as intrusions in his field of vision, but allowing them instead to permeate his being. There they may stand side by side with the others, to which he had accorded perennial truth, but which would perish without these grotesque additions.

It is important, then, to place the conclusion of *Remembrance* within the perspective not merely of time past, which is its most evident frame of reference, but of the one yet to come. The future is seemingly of scant relevance in the narrator's preoccupations, for his chief interest remains the preservation of the past, its delicacy and what once was the blossoming of his hopes. Yet the future is intricately linked with those hopes and it is, in reality, the main focus in his search for artistic expression. That explains what might otherwise appear as a surprising animosity against the signs of old age that he suddenly detects all around him. They represent an encroachment onto his vision, not of a simple past as much as of the future itself. It is what one might call the future of the past that concerns him. He senses the danger of succumbing to a present already touched by death, of foundering into the realm of nothingness. Gradually then a fuller meaning of old age is delineated. It is that of an existential present which demands keen awareness and a measure of choice.

Old age in the Proustian world is a stepping-stone either to death or to a new life. If Marcel is not to slip into it passively as most of those present at the party have done, he must use it to his own ends in the battle for survival. Age must then be considered the enemy, and as such it is transformed into a two-headed monster. Old age acquires the shape of all his unavowed fears, deforming and twisting everything it touches. If he is to triumph over it, he must fully appreciate its force. Hence his willful unmasking of all concealed signs of its presence, his elaboration on the distortions wrought by it upon limbs and faces. He proceeds no longer with the complacency of someone who thinks himself impervious to its undermining faculty, but with the rage of those who refuse to surrender.

It is in this context that the presentation of the aged people at the Guermantes' reception must be seen. It may seem cruel of Marcel to dwell so disproportionately on the scars of old age, on the vacant stares, the bulbous noses, the strident voices. His is in reality a mechanism of defense that gradually takes over, a manner of buttressing himself against the temptation of acquiescence to the ravages of time. In keeping with the best tradition of defense, he turns to the offensive. Pitilessly, he looks for hidden signs, so as not to be lulled by any reassuring appearance.

Age cannot be appraised solely in terms of skin and muscle deterioration, of course. Those are merely the more obvious signs of a generally diminishing vitality. The figures that are conjured up are intrusions upon the beauty he cherishes—not of traits alone but of values more complex and spiritual. Is it the sight of age in itself, truly, that brings nausea to Marcel? Or is it not, rather, the void it reveals, the barren souls that are suddenly and indecently exposed, now that all pleasing contours have been consumed by time? The inferred answer contained in the latter of these two questions not only justifies but also makes imperative Marcel's revulsion against the display of the flesh's dominance upon the life of individuals. For aging in the great salon where he ventures after a long absence, is an unmasking, a forcible removal of a pleasing exterior donned during the brief frolicking that was youth. One remembers that the narrator's grandmother remains movingly beautiful to the end, with her wisps of white hair blown by the wind upon her brow. But she was whole, with deep integrity ruling her life from within. Her nature did not assign a minor role to the yearnings of the spirit. The people at the Guermantes' party, on the other hand, have no such inner beauty, and the withering of their flesh removes the last vestige of what had constituted their appeal. The pitiless vision of old age denounces the flimsy world of a moribund aristocracy to reveal its inherent depravity.

Marcel has learned a lesson from his contemplation of old age displayed for him like portraits of ancestors. What he has meditated in these long moments transcends the immediate present and is slowly joined to an immutable past, as if those people were already dead, as if he could see his own death. But he no longer watches the shadows before him as if they were menacing to his own survival. He has learned that his memories can spring back to life. They can ally themselves with the laws of time and assume its very shape.

> Then I thought that that morning which . . . had given me at the same time the idea of my opus and the fear of not being able to realize it, would above all imprint upon it the shape that I had once sensed in the Combray church, and which usually remains invisible, that of Time (pp. 1044–45).

Thus it is that old age, perceived by Marcel in gruesome contortions at the Guermantes' reception, will have proven an inspiration for the resurrection of life through art.

8

LIFE/DEATH: A JOURNEY (YASUNARI KAWABATA)

By Bettina L. Knapp

[In Yasunari Kawabata's novel The Master of Go, *we see a Japan of the 1930's, hovering between antiquity and a modernity which affects even the ancient ritual of the stylized Go competition itself. "In old times the holder of the title," Kawabata explains, "fearful of doing injury to it, seems to have avoided real competition even in practice matches. Never before, probably, was there a master who fought a title match at the advanced age of sixty-four.*[1] *But in the future the existence of a master who did not play would be unthinkable. Shusai the Master would seem, in a variety of meanings, to have stood at the boundary between the old and the new" (p. 53). Veneration for the age and status of the Master would have given him an advantage in the title game were it not for modern regulations. "The game of Go tended to be controlled these (new) days by inflexible rules. Elaborate conditions had been set for the Master's last game, to keep his old-fashioned willfulness under control, to deny him a special status, to ensure complete equality." As Professor Knapp shows, such had not been the traditional Japanese way.*

That the Master is not only old, but also ill, is a factor in the match which is the central event of The Master of Go. *His 30-year-old opponent, Otaké, reveres the Master but must re-*

main an opponent if he is to play out the match. Otaké's patience is taxed on several occasions because the managers of the game do allow the ailing Master certain concessions, and when he learns of the gravity of the older man's illness, he nearly forfeits the game. But Shusai the Master never becomes a mere object of pity. He holds his own. "The Master was able to forget his own illness when he sat down at the board, and Otaké, struggling himself to forget, was at a disadvantage. The Master had become a tragic figure" (p. 103). Indeed, the Master faces death throughout the tournament, as the reader is always reminded. Chapters describing the last game alternate with the journalist-narrator's flash-forwards to when the Master will have died. He describes his photographs of the deceased Master's face, for example. These seem to the narrator unreal since they capture neither life nor death, but suggest both.

Such existential ambiguity, hovering between this life and the next, is equally striking in The Sound of the Mountain. *There another man in his 60's, Shingo, remains alive for the duration of the novel, but his mortality seems quite as immediate as that of the Master, Shusai. Although aging, he remains the patriarch of his family. Family funds, power, and decisions are in his hands. Nothing in this is unusual in Japanese society. It is his internal life which is of interest. Temperamentally, he is at odds with his wife but in harmony with his daughter-in-law.*

Shingo spends a good deal of time reminiscing, perhaps because of his awareness of the onset of age and of death. Early in the novel, he fantasized that he would like to turn his head in for a cleaning, like laundry, because he sometimes felt muddled. Less humorously, he is struck by a newspaper article in which it is stated, "People ought to go away while they still are loved." Like other aging people, Shingo finds himself awakening early in the morning. He dreams of death and is frightened by "the sound of the mountain" which seems to beckon him to the beyond. He fears death. Dreams are important to him and to the novel. They form part of its atmosphere of revery, which expresses the beginning of loss of memory in Shingo. His thoughts are sometimes vague, sometimes beautifully medita-

tive. For all their haziness, they make sense, and he uses them to understand himself.

In keeping with the ageless, cyclical quality of the Japanese view of time characterized so well by Bettina Knapp, the novel ends without a strong sense of closure. We know that Shingo—and the other characters, for that matter—will die as we all will. But it is rather as if he will fade into the landscape to become the stuff of another's dreams. Aging gracefully while keeping dignity and respect would seem to be a Japanese specialty.

Indirectly, perhaps even through contrast, The Sound of the Mountain's *serene answers lead the Western reader to raise some practical questions. If integrity means, in the Eriksonian sense, the resolve to maintain what one wishes to keep in one's personality and to transcend those values which have come to seem inadequate, can an old person achieve integrity despite the failings of memory? For Shingo, dreams and memory are helpful in sorting out reality, it seems. But more generally, the reader may ask, how real is the self-acceptance which a truly forgetful old person may achieve? The bland and perhaps cruel answer is that senility may be nature's kindness. Nietzsche wrote: "Memory says, I did that. Pride says, I could not have done that. Eventually, memory yields." But for the Eastern mind, I suspect that the questions and answers may be different. Facing death's approach seems to be not a quest for self-acceptance, but rather the acceptance that one will soon merge anonymously with the cosmos—Eds.]*

IN ZEN BUDDHIST, Taoist, and Shintoist traditions, which are implicit in the Japanese experience, existence is viewed as a totality and not in terms of a loss or gain, past or present, youth or age. Life and death are part of a process, as attested to by the following statement made by a 15th-century Zen Buddhist monk, "I take a rest as I switch from the path of suffering to the path of enlightenment; if it rains, let it! If the wind blows, let it!"[1] Life is considered metaphorically by the Japanese as a journey between the world of illusion—implying the full range from suffering to serenity—and the release of death. They are not separate entities; each is experienced in the other's realm in relative degrees of purpose and power.

"The eternal traveler" was the epithet ascribed to Yasunari Kawabata (1899–1972), the author of *The Master of Go* and *The Sound of the Mountain*, two novels expressive of the Japanese attitude toward life and death. The phrase was well suited to Kawabata. When composing his works, he was in the habit of wandering about Japan from inn to inn. His so-called "rootlessness" was a paradigm of metaphysical notions deeply impressed in Zen Buddhism, Taoism, and Shintoism. The notion of flux at the heart of these philosophical concepts is expressed in the temperaments of the two old protagonists of the novels mentioned above. They face old age not with fear or desolation, but as part of a natural transforming rite.

Life is not ego-centered, as in the Western view; existence is a series of fleeting moments. Life and death are accepted in the rotating pattern of universal flux. Whereas mind, matter, and time are conceived by the Westerner as something tangible, the Zen Buddhist considers them as unreal. Nothing is permanent for him because continuity and duration do not exist. Cyclical and nonlinear time schemes predominate. There is no past, no future. The only concrete reality is the *moment* or *actuality*.

The Oriental, therefore, does not disavow or fear the aging process. It is no more to be conquered than nature; it is not to be rejected or reviled. Each stage of life, lived in its plenitude, arouses wonderment, entails its own dignity, and merits the compassion or admiration befitting it. The phenomenon of humankind, whether revealed in a young and beautiful body or in an old one, even in a dead one, as in a skull, is used to convey man's connection with nature. No distinction, therefore, is to be made between one form of life and another: "the plants and trees, the land itself, shall all attain Buddhahood."[2] Man is—as is a flower, tree, mountain—an emanation of totality. To drink a drop of sea water is to have imbibed from all the oceans.

The Master of Go is a reportage, a combination of autobiography, memoir, and journalism. Kawabata was present at the Go match (1938) which he covered for the Osaka and Tokyo newspapers. The events are authentic, although the names are changed, save that of the Zen Master. They revolve around the "invincible" Go Master who, now old and a victim of heart disease, loses his last championship and dies shortly thereafter.

Kawabata neither feels sorry for the Go Master during his terminal match nor does the protagonist himself express terror at his defeat or approaching death. To fear death is to be bound to a host of superstitions, Kawabata intimates. It is to be paralyzed, to be unable to live life fully in each of its manifestations.

That Kawabata chooses a game as the pivotal force around which he constructs his novel, is significant. Games indicate struggle; a way of pitting man's actions and reasoning power against another; a means of determining his place in life; a need to risk momentary supremacy. Played on a circumscribed board, the game is an expression of man's limited liberty. As life is made up of complex acts and modes, so a game, in reduced context, also depends upon infinite combinations of plays in finite time. Games also instill order into anarchical situations, substituting a thinking and objective realm for a more primitive and instinctual world.[3] The game of Go takes on the aura of a sacred rite. The black and white stones in Go are charged entities, filled with the energy the players invest into them. Hierophanies of sorts, these sacred objects are metaphors, recipients of intense thought, mute actors rejecting or participating in the cosmic flow. The motility of the players' thoughts, as conveyed in the black and white stones, replicates the philosophical notion of perpetual change. The game of Go is both a *rite de sortie* (the manner chosen by the Master to exit from the world of humankind into another realm) and a *rite d'entrée* for his opponent (who will be assuming the Master's position with its distinction and its responsibilities). To emphasize the notion of fluidity in life, as well as the eternity of time, the beginning and conclusion of *The Master of Go* are virtually the same: both refer to the Master's death at the age of sixty-seven at the Urokoya Inn at Atami on January 18, 1940.

The novel gravitates around the Go moves. Nearly every

chapter of the forty-one composing the novel either begins with a specific move or refers to one or more. Whether the moves are those made by the Master or Otaké, each is described in terms of the game itself, but expanded as well, to include the psychic and physical states, the personality and environment of those participating in this universal experience.

The Master's physical state, for example, is drawn in great detail, as is that of his opponent. Carefully, objectively described, the Master's eyes, eyebrows, lips, and strands of hair come to the forefront each in turn and are imbued with a life of their own before being integrated into a complex totality. The Master's eyelids are swollen and his speech is slow "as if to relieve the heaviness in the air" (p. 6). Each move he makes takes him through time in seconds, minutes, hours; with the keenness of youth and the deliberateness of age. When the Master's eyelids close, linear time seems to vanish; during long periods of meditation, when he hears the Lotus Sutra inwardly, he sways gently to the rhythm of its monotonous incantations. The slowness of the Master's play is indicative of his detachment from this world.

The narrator describes the Master as having so little flesh on his body that he resembles an "undernourished child" (p. 19). Such images, depicting the smallness of his frame as well, indicate the life force slowly withdrawing its heat and energetic powers from him as from a barren branch. But the Master does not always give the impression of diminution or finitude. When seated, for example, next to the Go board, he seems to grow in dimension and power. The confidence he has in his art—the concentration of the emotions needed for the struggle within the game proper—the activity of his mental powers resulting from the protracted periods of intense observation and discipline, serve to increase his stature. His jaw then seems stronger, his trunk longer, his face wider (p. 20).

Delineated by Kawabata in sharp brush strokes, the Master is seated in front of the Go board at the outset of his last match, attentive, intensely concentrated in his mental combat. Reminiscent of a Noh figure, he holds a prop in his hand—a fan—which simultaneously reflects his exhaustion and his aggressivity. His energy is slow to crystallize, but powerful.

Whenever the Master began a match, Kawabata writes, he seemed "to exude a quiet fragrance that cooled and cleaned the air around him" (p. 35). The "House of Autumn Leaves" in which the Go game is being played reflects nature: the sliding doors and panels are painted with maple leaves, evergreens, and dahlias. After the beginning ceremonies and plays, the game grows more involved and, concomitantly, the Master's breathing accelerates.

> Yet there was nothing to suggest disorder. The waves that passed through his shoulders were quite regular. They were to me like concentration of violence, or the doings of some mysterious power that had taken possession of the Master (p. 39).

Virtually closed to the exterior world, the Master sits uncommunicative, his face expressionless. Then as suddenly as he seems to have retreated from the workaday world, so he returns to it. A mood of repose fills the atmosphere. The Master's breathing returns to normal. The face is at ease. The change which seemed to have been experienced deeply by the Master is so sudden, so unexpected, that the narrator wonders whether he has witnessed "the workings of the Master's soul." Alive, the Master's eyes dance; all aspects of his physiognomy express that moment of exquisite intuition when the passage of enlightenment makes itself felt and the soul casts off "all sense of identity and the fires of combat" (p. 40).

Otakó, in contrast to the Master, moves about, jokes, indulges in conversation. The dignity the Master exhibits has come with age. Otakó still feels hindrances, fears, joys and does not know how to adapt to these. He has not yet transcended the duality of the phenomenological world, nor has he experienced the emptiness and fullness of being. Plenitude can be known in the smallest activities of life—when looking at the moon's rays float on water or observing a cherry blossom imprinting configurations upon a blank horizon, its radiant perfection mirrored in the empty sky. The Master in his quiet, although tense way, understands nature's movements; he has experienced *satori*, when intuition allows one to perceive the mysteries of nature, a vaster reality beyond form. Once the Master had "sunk himself into a session" he did not stir from the board (p. 42). Each of the moves is weighted, its dualities savored.

The rituals of ablution and purification are followed during the course of the game, bringing sanctity to the entire arena. The Master balks against modernization, particularly as applied to the Go game.

> It may be said that the Master was plagued in his last match by modern rationalism, to which fussy rules were everything, from which all the grace and elegance of Go as art had disappeared, which quite dispensed with respect for elders and attached no importance to mutual respect as human beings. From the way of Go the beauty of Japan and the Orient had fled (p. 52).

The Master did not blame Otaké for the intrusion of Western logistics: these were symptomatic of a dying way of life, of the winning of the East by the West. "In a day the spirit of which was a mixture of idolatry and iconoclasm, the Master went into his last match as the last survivor among idols of old" (p. 53). The Master is reminiscent of the Samurai—and his Bushido credo—willing to give up his life at any moment when awareness of the circularity of existence called for it. The ease, as well as the pain, marking the transformatory process would be blunted and become an exquisitely felt impression.

As the match progresses the Master grows weaker. He develops breathing difficulties; palpitations come upon him in shorter intervals. He is bathed in perspiration; discomfort follows. Yet, the Master does not let go. He plays other games during the long intervals between moves: chess, Mahjong, billiards. His mind has to be full. In that way not a single thought can disturb the precarious balance which hovers between the empty and filled squares. His mind, no longer the finely attuned instrument, is given to moods, to struggle. Only by outer effort—the playing of other games—can he quiet the tension.

Go pursued its course: attacks and counter-attacks, parrying and dodging, frontal, side, rear confrontations. The board is filled with stones on one corner, empty on another. Energy, forced into the very center of the board, radiates in multiple patterns.

The last few moves prior to the finale are enacted with heightened awareness, determined perseverence, and greater order, that "of a precisely tooled machine, a relentless mathematical progression" (p.174). Never do the Master's eyes leave the center of action. Increasingly anxious, he declares, "I think I would like if possible to finish today" (p.172). The Master's struggle is condensed, his breathing again rapid. The most minute nuances of facial expression and gesture are contained and stilled beneath his mask. His attention span lapses, and anguish seems to predominate. The observer commented that "White" was having difficulties. The match is a metaphor for age struggling against youth, antiquity opposed to modernity. The Master loses the game, and dies soon after. He completed the circularity of his existence with his last match, but he also exposed to the world the personality of a man "so disciplined in an art that he had lost the better part of reality" (p.32).

Whereas *The Master of Go* focused on the patriarchal sphere almost exclusively, *The Sound of the Mountain* encompasses female principles as well. Rather than in the world of the game, the polarities of life are now experienced in daily activities. Moods float in and out of the novel in spectacularly lyrical visualizations. Feelings clothe the protagonists more powerfully in *The Sound of the Mountain* than in *The Master of Go*. Since more emphasis is given to the female principle, Nature (a metaphor for this fruitful and productive element) is depicted in far greater detail than in *The Master of Go*.

The tale is set in Kamakura for its great temples and the wondrous Diabutsu (The Great Buddha); the entire area, surrounded by mountains, is like a giant park. The presence of Buddha is felt in the novel's atmosphere, as if lighting the way both spiritually and existentially.

Shingo, the grandfather, is portrayed in depth from the very outset of the novel. His presence is the radiating force: as an experience, a memory, an image or part of a complex of personality factors. "He wore an air of thought" (p.3) Kawabata writes, as though trying to recall something, to evoke a transient feeling which was as material and as heavy as a garment. Shingo's age is stated as a "cycle of sixty years" (p.6), thus emphasizing the non-linear time scheme so precious to the Oriental psyche. To mark his advanced years and perhaps his decline, the author notes that Shingo began spitting up blood and that his son, Shuichi, had suggested that he consult a doctor. When Shingo refused, his son declared that such an attitude was symptomatic of old age.

Shingo is aware of his age. His teeth have grown bad. Only one age-related factor really annoys him—his insomnia. But then, he reasons, his wakefulness is caused by his wife's snoring. Yasuko, sixty-three years old, is the one who awakens him. At night, when he lies in bed, his eyes wide open, the moon shines brightly in its "vast depth" (p.7). It is then that he feels his loneliness most powerfully; it is also at this time that Nature impresses itself upon him. He listens to its voices which speak from the garden: "the screeching of the insects," the cherry tree imperceptibly wafting its branches slowly his way; the mosquitoes buzzing; the leaf drinking the cool waters of dawn.

Nature is receptive and fertile; it becomes the recipient for Shingo's feelings, conveying sensations of tranquility or anguish. Mountain, flower, tree, sand patterns, stones, a dead branch or solitary bird, each aspect of nature becomes an image of man's aloofness and evokes a sense of awe.

Shingo listens at night to "the sound of the mountain." He hears it murmur with a twinge of fear. For the Japanese, the mountain has multiple meanings. It represents verticality, communication between earth and heaven. Mountains are closest to the sky and seem imbued with spiritual purity. Monasteries were and still are located in mountains—on Mt. Fuji—allowing the acolyte to participate directly in nature, experience its birds and animals, dip into its crystal pools of water, glide along its rocks. Intuitively, the spirit of these natural forces—the *kami*—emerges; its impact upon the believer stimulates his sensations, allowing him to participate in the giant cosmic awakening of which he is a part.

Shingo, reminiscent of the wandering and solitary Zen monks, looks deeply into the heart of the mountain from his room. Divested of unessential sensations, he grasps the very heart of the mountain, as though he were a modern counterpart of the great Sesshu (1420–1506), an artist whose landscape paintings reflected the range and depth of human feeling, imposing upon the onlooker intimations of cosmic serenity. Shingo also experiences the universe in feelings of emptiness and solitude, in the vastness of an unlimited expanse which seems to penetrate his window and the heart of his own being.

Although Shingo senses his isolation, and his solitude increases every time he looks out of his window at the mountains surrounding Kamakura, he also feels strengthened in his oneness with the universe. When a shadow cast by the moon comes upon him, he responds to it as if it were a blanket of warmth brought his way. "It was a windless night. The moon was near full, in the moist, sultry air the fringe of trees that outlined the mountain was blurred. They were motionless, however" (p.8). Calm and stillness fill the atmosphere. "Not a leaf on the fern by the veranda was stirring. In these mountain recesses of Kamakura the sea could sometimes be heard at night" (p.8). Shingo wonders whether he is confusing the sound of the sea with that of the mountain. The sound ceases. A chill passes over Shingo's body. The mountain seems to alter in tone and consistency. It moves in his mind's eye, patterning itself after slow breathing, a weakening of universal force. He wonders whether this is an intimation of his demise. He probes the sensations which have stirred within him. Thoughts of his past intrude. The image of the woman he once loved impresses itself incisively in his mind's eye; he had loved his wife's sister but she died long before he married. The image of this spectral beauty in all of her tenderness haunts him still.

Shingo and his son, Shuichi, work in the same business firm in Tokyo. They also live in the same house in Kamakura. Shuichi, married for only two years to Kikuko, is already unfaithful. It is for Kikuko that Shingo feels great empathy. At sunrise daily, it is Kikuko who alights from her bed in simple and earthy beauty to brew the morning tea. He watches her as she moves about, the "slight but beautiful way she had of moving her shoulders" (p.16). She is reminiscent of an Utamaro painting, of one of those beautiful eighteenth-century women whose garments and features the painter emphasized by molding contours in infinitely delicate curves. Shingo's eye rests on Kikuko and follows her body in seemingly endless circles. The family notices how tender Shingo is with Kikuko. For him, indeed, she is "a window looking out of a gloomy house." She brings relief from a painfully oppressive atmosphere. Kikuko never makes negative remarks concerning Shingo's age, never insinuates what his own son referred to as a loss of memory or other weaknesses. She draws comfort from what she considers to be his wisdom, his orderly ways, his stable views. For his part, he is sympathetically aware of her grim marital life.

Fusako, Shingo's daughter, has just returned to the family. Her marriage has soured. She brings her two children with her: a four-year-old and an infant. Fusako not only complains continuously about her wayward husband, but she is also deeply hurt by her father's lack of affection for her. "It amounts to cruelty," she declares (p.45). Shingo dreams frequently of what life would have been had he married the one he had truly loved. Fusako, then, would never have been born.

During the New Year's celebration at Atami, where the firm was giving a party, Shingo notes that his hair is growing white. Concomitantly, he observes a winter cherry tree blooming and feels "as if he had come upon spring in a wholly different world" (p.106). Fascinated by the cherry blossoms "as they were reflected by the pond," he experiences their closeness as if penetrating eternity itself. Crossing a small foot bridge in the garden, a tree—umbrella-shaped, so covered is it with red blossoms—seems to beckon him. He is overcome with nausea, distress and disquietude. His temples and forehead throb. He is not yet ready for death. His mission in life has not yet been completed.

Shingo is depicted cutting down the cherry blossoms in the spring in his own garden. In a few masterful words, reminiscent of Zen paintings of the fifteenth-century Josetsu and Shubun, Kawabata describes how Shingo must cut off the roots that threaten to stifle the plant. So powerful has the cherry tree grown that it nearly takes over the garden. The thought of falling blossoms, associated with death, and a world stripped bare of foliage and greenness, mirrors the march of linear time. People should die, Shingo's wife murmurs, when they are still loved and not wait until they become a burden, unable to function.

Many of Shingo's friends have died and much of his time is spent attending funerals and in trying to think back to the time when he knew the people in question. One dream in particular torments him so much that he tells his wife about it. The dream concerns a dead friend who offers him noodles which he eats. If you eat food offered by a dead person, he wonders, does it predict your own demise? (p.39). For Shintoists, the spirits of ancestors are alive and about, and usually visit the living in sanctuaries as well as in dreams. Interestingly enough, the man who offered Shingo the noodles was a cabinet maker, an artisan of the "old school" (p.31), thereby representative of tradition, and a man in whose presence Shingo felt at ease.

Such dreams, as well as others, are pivotal in his life. They permit him to transform what had been a completely passive attitude toward the family situation into a relatively active one. After discovering the facts concerning his son's mistress, and following his ill-favored daughter's return home, Shingo decides he needs distracting and goes dancing with one of the office girls, Eiko. Shingo knows that she will be the one to introduce him to Shuichi's mistress, that he will have to be instrumental in severing his son's liaison. Once he has returned home, again thoughts of dead friends flash into Shingo's mind. A few nights later Shingo attends a funeral in Tokyo and dreams about Matsushima Bay. There are pine trees in his vision, surrounding crystal waters, shedding their deep greenness over the entire landscape. He holds a young girl in his arms. She is unknown. The dream reflects his profound need for tenderness. This dream is replicated in a reverie on the train going to Tokyo. As the train speeds by he observes two special pine trees emerging from a grove. He sees them not simply as impersonal objects, but as acting and reacting to each other. "They leaned toward each other, as if they were about to embrace. The branches came so near that it was as if they might embrace at any moment" (p.166).

Increasingly disturbed by his son's escapades, his drunkenness, and particularly distressed by the change he notes in

Kikuko's behavior, Shingo discovers that Kikuko has had an abortion. She cannot stand the thought of bringing her husband's child into the world, not while he has a mistress. She goes to her family in Kyoto. Some weeks pass. Shingo contacts her. He cannot bear the thought of his son's misdeeds. Again on the train going to Tokyo he spies the same two trees which had been embracing in an earlier vision. Now, in May, they look different, set against a glazed sky and sparkling air.

> The pines were no longer just pines. They were entangled with the abortion. Perhaps he would always be reminded of it when he passed them to and from work (p.185).

He meets Kikuko in the Shinjuku park and asks her to return to Kamakura and live with them. She agrees. It is as if she were just emerging from behind a shaded tree. The little bridge set on the lake, with its stone lantern, surrounded by the irregular patterned stones, the neatly planted bushes, the perfectly raked gravel, symbolize the onset of a life for Kikuko, who is finally coming into her own as she steps out into the sunlight bathing the park.

Shingo is moved by the beauty of the surroundings. "It has brought you to life, Father," Kikuko says gently (p.189). She knows that greenness, growth, fertility, activity will allow vitality to flow into his aged frame. They walk together next to the bed of white flowers, observing the gentle curves of the tulip tree, its branches bowing deeply toward the earth.

Shingo returns home. He suggests that Shuichi and Kikuko move out and start their own home, but they refuse. Fusako also wants to remain there; she suggests that her father help her and Kikuko open a small business. Shingo will have to meditate upon it; as patriarch, his influence is important. It has not diminished with age. He is tranquil as he withdraws into his room for the night and there lies awake, gazing out of his window onto his garden. Serenity permeates his being as he prepares himself for the journey between the earthly and the cosmic world.

9

OLD AGE AND THE MODERN LITERARY IMAGINATION

By Barbara and Allan Lefcowitz

[This rich and original chapter examines how modern writers from many countries "have incorporated the bound and static nature of old age into literary fictions whose forms we expect to turn upon movement, open-endedness, and change." For the first time that we know of in literary criticism, they propose a detailed typology of old people as literary characters, with ample illustrations. Their four types are:

1) Models of stoical endurance.

2) Touchstones revealing the moral deficiencies of present society in general, or of its younger members in particular.

3) Symptoms of an oppressive society or of spiritual stagnation.

4) Magnifying mirrors for the absurdity of life itself, "a tale told by an idiot, full of sound and fury, signifying nothing."

The Lefcowitzes share our belief that "there is no simple chronological thread through the maze of ambivalence and variety that masks the narrative shaping of old age in literature." The wealth of their presentation raises many questions which should stimulate future research into literary characters. Their categories tend to fall entirely into the division of illustrative characters (those designed to point up an idea), to the exclusion of esthetic (those used to move the plot) or mimetic ones ("round" characters, who possess contrasting traits and who evolve).[1] *Nor do they mention characters, like those of Proust, whose development is followed by their author from youth or maturity to old age. Such character depiction implies an acceptance of the life cycle by the implied author. In short, the categories used here do not fully reflect how free and how self-actualizing old people may be. Does literature ever do so?*

The esthetic function of aged characters—a more superficial role than those discussed in this chapter—is frequently that of adversary, the "blocking character" in the classical comedy of Ancient Rome and of Europe, who frustrates the desires of the young. In melodrama and popular literature, this adversary attains the exalted status of the ancient fiend whose enormous wisdom and long-accumulated resources are pitted against the younger hero (Tolkien's Sauron; Count Dracula; Fu Manchu). Other esthetic functions of the aged are those of the dupe, the passive recipient of actions designed to defraud him or her, like the title character of Balzac's Cousin Pons, *who thus unwittingly motivates the action. Finally, the person depicted as moving through a full life cycle creates a satisfying sense of closure, like the hero of the story "Johnny Pye and the Fool-Killer" by Stephen Vincent Benét.*

The old person as mimetic character typically moves from isolation and self-absorption to openness, giving, and a new capacity for love, combining in one the virtues of generativity and solidarity. Such are Scrooge in Charles Dickens' A Christmas Carol; *Ichmenyev in Dostoevsky's* The Insulted and the Injured; *and the aging heroes of Ingmar Bergman's film "Wild Strawberries," or of "On Golden Pond." Depiction of the old woman as mimetic character often has feminist features since she frees herself, or demonstrates her freedom, from the domination of male-oriented society and finds new and surprising avenues toward self-actualization—see the films "The Shameless Old Lady" or "Harold and Maude."*

Even when they are illustrative, the "touchstone" characters of the Lefcowitzs' categorization are often enriched by changes in the ways that others perceive them in many works. At first, presented from the viewpoint of the naive observer, such old people appear to be eccentric, frightening, silly—or all three at once. Gradually they reveal themselves as wise and kind. The accumulated experience of such characters is often glorified by the implied author to the extent that they become otherwordly, like the popularized versions of Merlin the Magician; the Great Owl and the mouse "Mr. Ages" in the animated film, "The Secret of N.I.M.H."; or the angels who except for God are no doubt among the oldest characters in all of literature—Mrs. Who, Mrs. Which, and Mrs. Whatsit in Madeleine L'Engle's A Wrinkle in Time. *Such figures partake of the fairytale experience designed to inculcate children painlessly and engagingly with moral values.*[2] *In the instances cited here, the moral is that the old are rich in helpful advice and should be respected. Consider the clear examples of the benevolent old Jedi knight Obi-Wan Kenobi and his friend Yoda in the "Star Wars" films. Although our dominant medium of communication may have changed from literature to television and film, we have not dropped the golden thread of our folk-cultural heritage which is our reverence for old age—Eds.]*

> . . . if an old man is dealt with in his subjective aspect he is not a good hero for a novel; he is finished, set, with no hope, no development to be looked for . . . nothing that can happen to him is of any importance.
>
> —Simone de Beauvoir, *The Coming of Age*

OLD PEOPLE ENDURE; old people cling to outworn beliefs and lifestyles; old people embody the loss of power and options, entropy rather than energy. If they move at all, it is usually toward greater physical and mental decline, or regressively toward recapture of a past that is likely to be highly idealized. We expect fiction and drama, on the other hand, to unfold toward some sort of *telos* whether internalized or overt; action, discovery, and surprise are the *sine qua non* of their condition, even if the ultimate discovery is one of marked disillusion. Yet despite the surface paradox, writers do deal with old people and have done so from the beginning.

Our main concern here will be with sketching various ways in which nineteenth- and twentieth-century writers have incorporated the bound and static nature of old age into literary fictions whose forms we expect to turn upon movement, openendedness, and change. When we take into account the social and economic stress upon progress, or at least change, that has marked western society since the industrial revolution, any literary embodiment of mere stasis would seem to be particularly difficult to portray, except as an object of denigration. Certainly old age itself no longer inspires veneration in a society where economic productivity is a supreme value, where easily available written records have long since supplanted the historical value of a long oral memory, where the power of the authoritarian family is, for better or worse, rapidly eroding, and where magic (once the province of the wise old man or woman) is now funneled through wires and called technology, or dispensed by physicians of the soul, either on the street or in sanitized offices.

We will focus on four different patterns of narrative response to the static condition of old age. Without challenging the cultural devaluation of old age, the first portrays old people as models, despite—or possibly because of—their set natures. In these narratives such characters usually embody the qualities of stoicism and endurance, and often live in rural settings. Their resignation to the loss of power intrinsic to old age may reflect an author's wish to deny or soften the threatening power of a new social order; or endurance itself may serve as a counterweight to a writer's harbinger of personal mental breakdown.

A second pattern treats the old person as a touchstone or means of revealing the moral insufficiencies of younger members of a particular society. The same qualities of stoicism and the same tendencies toward sentimentalizing may be present here as in the first pattern, but the focus is not so much on the old person, who may hover godlike in the background, as on the light shed upon the delusions, petty greeds, and sputterings toward unattainable goals of other characters. Such idealized touchstone characters may illuminate the shortcomings of an entire social order.

In the third pattern of narrative response to old age, the characters are treated as symptoms of either an oppressive social order or an overall spiritual stagnation. Though they may not be denigrated, such old people are not idealized, and both physical and mental decay become permissible features of their fictive life. Regret may become the dominant tone—regret for lost opportunities or for the inability of a person to grasp from his dwindling hoard of days anything more than an intensification of feelings of loss and betrayal that previously were merely inchoate. If the author is committed to some notion of progress, either political or aesthetic, the old person may become a symptom of any obstacle to such progress or to the life force itself, as in the tradition of the *senex iratus* (the chronically angry and complaining old person).

Finally, some writers use the old as a magnifying mirror of the absurdity of life itself. Aesthetically, an old person is a logical choice for the delineation of such a satirical vision: if life is absurd, causality and progress are illusions; stasis *is* the ultimate reality rather than a disturbing contradiction or temporary obstacle to a goal's fulfillment in time. And if life is a grotesque joke, how better to embody that joke than by peopling one's stage with the senile and decrepit? The useless old become a comment on and reflection of our useless condition.

These patterns are by no means mutually exclusive nor intended to be exhaustive. Though historical factors will be taken into account, we will not attempt to force either the patterns themselves or examples within the patterns into chronological order, largely because we believe there is no simple chronological thread through the maze of ambivalence and variety that marks the narrative shaping of old age in literature.

1. Old Person as Model

In "Resolution and Independence" the perseverance of the stone-like leechgatherer, "the oldest man . . . that ever wore grey hairs," not only helps relieve Wordsworth's despondency, but impresses itself upon his mind as a moral talisman. Almost 140 years later, Eudora Welty writes in "A Worn Path" about the heroic determination of old Phoenix Jackson to work her way through the thorn and animal-ridden woods in order to get medicine for her ailing grandson. Phoenix persists on her errand despite the need to cross a dangerous bog, despite the advice of a hunter she meets, despite the fear engendered by a ghost-like scarecrow, and most significantly, despite the possibility that the objective purpose of her trip has no basis in reality: though Phoenix doesn't consciously ponder the issue, her grandson may indeed be long dead.

In a recent comment on the story's most ambiguous point: is the grandson really alive? Welty claims that it doesn't really matter, because Phoenix's "persisting in her landscape was the real thing, and the first and the real were what I wanted and worked to keep."[2] Later in the same commentary, Welty makes explicit the link between Phoenix's mission and the missions of all writers:

> The way to get there is the all-important, all-absorbing problem, and this problem is your reason for undertaking the story. . . . Like Phoenix, you work all your life to find your way, through all the obstructions and the false appearances and the upsets you may have brought on yourself, to reach a meaning— . . . And finally, too, like Phoenix, you have to assume that what you are working in aid of is life, not death.[3]

The question remains, of course, why an *old* person? Would not the endurance of, say, a crippled, blind, or poor person have sufficed as well for an analogue of the creative spirit? What is distinctive about the perseverance of an old person is the fact that he or she persists despite awareness of a severely limited time frame, an awareness that differs sharply from the vague recognition, "someday I will die," common to human beings of any age. The only comparable situation would be the time-consciousness of a younger person with a terminal illness, but even here the situation, while not lacking in opportunities for heroic action, would generally lack the special quality of endurance, that hardening of the will across a long period of time.

At least for Eudora Welty, then, the set nature of an old person becomes not an obstacle to narrative development, but the very stuff of its unfolding. Phoenix's personality and opportunities for objective success may be set, but her very boundedness provides the thrust for a ritual journey toward a goal which is simultaneously illusory and real, making her a most appropriate model for the creative artist. Despite the limits of time, energy, and awareness, the artist pushes through to an insight whose *imaginative* reality compensates for the shadowy nature of its objective references. The model is, then, both moral and aesthetic.

The line between an old person's perseverance and his resignation is a thin one, but even the more negative quality of resignation can provide a powerful model for a contemporary writer like Solzhenitsyn. In his novella, "Matryona's House", the protagonist is a superstitious old peasant woman who combines a saintly dedication to the needs of others with an ability to resign herself to the most absurd frustrations of the Russian bureaucratic system. Consistently her selflessness goes unrewarded, however, and even the narrator, who becomes a boarder in her cottage, takes her for granted, admitting: "For my part, I only saw Matryona as she was then, a lonely old woman. . . . "[4] When her relatives greedily conspire to dismantle a shed that adjoins her cottage—an act which signifies the ultimate assault on both Matryona's physical and spiritual reserves—the woman insists on helping to transport the timber, preferring to participate in her own dissolution rather than remain detached; by participating in the shed's destruction she can sustain her hold that much longer on her sole objective legacy.

During the preparations for transporting the logs, she annoys the narrator when she borrows and soils his quilted jacket. But after Matryona is killed, he begins to realize the pettiness of his reaction to the jacket incident and recognizes the saintly quality of the woman with whom he has boarded. Her combination of resignation, serenity, and perseverance—even unto her own destruction—takes on an allegorical quality, not so much of the strengths of Old Peasant Russia (though this, too is implied) but of the fleeting potential for goodness even in a world permeated by selfishness and stupidity:[5] "None of us who lived close to her perceived that she was that one righteous person without whom, as the saying goes, no city can stand. Neither can the whole world" (p.657).

While less an aesthetic than a moral model when compared to Phoenix Jackson, Matryona's existence becomes for the narrator-author a counterweight to his own doubts about the condition of modern society. Again, it is the very boundedness and hopelessness of an old person's condition that renders her a most suitable locus for a writer's attempt to objectify the quality of hope. From Matryona's boundedness grows Solzhenitsyn's own assertion of openness and possibility; from her resignation, ironically, grows his own renewal of determination. To have used a less bound and more dynamic protagonist would have stripped his narrative of much of its peculiar ironic power.

While an old person's graceful resignation to age itself—with an accompanying acceptance of the loss of personal power and of the passing of an obsolete social order—may not be as moving as an old person's resignation to fate, in its way it can also serve as a useful means of objectifying an author's uneasiness about his changing world. When Anthony Trollope published *Barchester Towers* in 1856, the tide of the times was moving "against favoritism and aristocratic insufficiency" and toward the awarding of positions through a civil service merit system,[6] the ascendency of public rather than church-controlled education, and the power of the middle class over the gentry: in short, against the complacent lifestyle of the Barchester clergy with its dependence on a private network of preferment. Such is the "spirit of the times" referred to by the aging Rev. Septimus Harding when he gracefully declines to accept an offer of Barchester's deanship:

> The truth is, I want the force of character which might enable me to stand against the spirit of the times. The call on all sides now is for young men, and I have not the nerve to put myself in opposition to the demand.[7]

Though Mr. Harding expresses a fleeting wish that he might have the power and will to fight against the new spirit, cheerful resignation to the absence of the requisite energy is the keynote of his response. Old age holds out its own rewards: "Every day that is added to my life increases my wish for peace and rest" (p.510).

Trollope does not, however, invest such a quiescent attitude with heroic trappings. Rather, at the close of the novel, he strikes a judicious Victorian balance between handwringing at the passing of the old order as embodied by Mr. Harding and a celebration of the latter's stance:

> The Author now leaves him in the hands of his readers; not as a hero, not as a man to be admired and talked of . . . but as a good man without guile, believing humbly in the religion which he has striven to teach, and guided by the precepts which he has striven to learn (p.545).

Granted, one wonders if anyone, even in the heyday of Barchesterian complacency, could ever be so flawlessly humble. But that is our cynicism. For Trollope, Mr. Harding's graceful acceptance of the decline that comes with age functions as a model, not so much for a way through the ravages of the human journey (as in our two previous examples) but for a way of meeting the last stage of the journey. The stasis of old age is not necessarily deplorable—provided, of course, that the character cheerfully accepts such a state, is not plagued by physical or mental symptoms of aging, and exists in a context where others, especially family members, treat him with warmth and compassion. And from the author's point of view, the static condition is not necessarily incompatible with the demands of narrative form—provided there is a rich supply of other characters (in this case, the newly promoted Quiverful and Arabin) who can supply a teleological counterthrust; and provided he can at the same time use his characters to express a slowly emerging awareness of the inevitable passing of the social order that is at the center of his work. More anguished responses to such threats will inform the work of later writers who use the same link between old age and social change.

II. Old Person as Touchstone

"They both have hearts of stone," Old Goriot cries on his deathbed in reference to the selfish daughters who blithely accepted his money and solicitude but could not muster sufficient gratitude to visit him during the final illness they helped to provoke. Throughout Balzac's novel, his bourgeois Lear serves to reveal the greed and materialism of a whole panoply of characters: his two daughters, the petty, handwringing Mme Vauquer, the sordid Vautrin, the socially ambitious and hence increasingly corruptible Rastignac, and a host of minor apostles of greed. Frequently we see Goriot playing the role of scapegoat as well, a role that harks back to one of the earliest social and literary responses to old people, dramatically revealing the petty cruelty of those who must resort to such actions in order to bolster their own shaky sense of power: "Then he had uses, too, as someone to snap at if they felt irritable, or try their wit on if they were in a good temper."[8]

Not that Goriot is a paradigm of either moral or spiritual virtue; his obsessive devotion to his daughters frequently edges into both the pathetic and the ridiculous. Even during his deathbed soliloquy he gilds his anguish with the illusion that he might have been spared his fate if only he had managed his money better. Yet if we take a relative measure of the citizenry of Balzac's Paris, Goriot's flawed virtue clearly wins the day. That such a deluded and pathetic person should serve as the author's most worthy character may indeed underscore the bitter irony of Balzac's social critique, but even a flawed touchstone is better than none at all.

Decline is a key factor in shaping Goriot's role as a touchstone. Through observing the literal decline of his income as he foolishly sacrifices his assets in order to enrich his daughters, we learn more about the stupidity of such figures as Mme Vauquer. Though the physical dissolution that accompanies aging is vividly evoked with references to Goriot's shrinking calves and leaden, graying eyes whose "red rims seemed to ooze blood" (p.53), the old man's decline is never merely exploited as an end in itself, but as part of a dramatic context where we can view other characters' responses to the signs of that decline. Thus does Balzac accomplish two feats: he is able to present the painful physical and mental aspects of aging without drowning his reader in morbid sentimentality; and simultaneously he demonstrates how it is possible to intertwine the very process of one character's decline with a narrative that moves constantly forward to excoriate the moral pretenses of Parisian society.

Though Goriot is at times mawkish and ludicrously obsessed, he always retains a sufficient core of humanity to resist those outer limits of eccentricity which would warrant placing him in the time-worn category of the old person as freak, although the use of markedly eccentric old characters can produce powerful moral reverberations and serve to create an aesthetic balance not otherwise attainable. Frank Norris' tough-minded, naturalistic novel, *McTeague,* contains a fine example of this process. Both Miss Baker, a morbidly shy retired dressmaker, and Grannis, an equally shy old Englishman who lives in an adjoining room of the boardinghouse, help to bring out the full implications of the greed-and-violence code followed by three of the novel's main characters: McTeague himself, the embittered dentist; Zerkow, the unscrupulous junkman; and Schouler, McTeague's jealousy-ridden antagonist. In contrast with the latter characters' greed, purposiveness, and susceptibility to violence, Grannis and Miss Baker lead quiet, parsimonious lives marked by rote dedication to a single innocuous activity—in the case of Miss Baker, making a cup of tea at precisely the same moment each afternoon, and in the case of Grannis, binding together pamphlets that he never reads. It is the aimlessness of Grannis' activity in particular that throws the naked ambition of the other characters into sharp relief. When asked why he binds the pamphlets, all he can manage is "I—I'm sure I can't quite say; a little habit, you know; a diversion, a—a—it occupies one, you know."[9]

In *McTeague* the two old people function dramatically to reinforce their position as touchstones. Eventually they come together to express their mutual admiration during an interlude between two of the novel's most violent disruptions of human love: the murder of Maria by the avaricious Zerkow, and McTeague's desertion of his wife, Trina, an act which leads ultimately to her murder as well. Though the union of Grannis and Miss Baker is couched in sentimental language, it stands out as the sole humane relationship in the entire novel: "They walked hand in hand in a delicious garden where it was always autumn" (p.228). Autumn and old age take on their own positive dynamic as the rest of Norris' fictive world moves toward annihilation. Ironically, in *McTeague's* sex- and money-driven world, the choral song of Oedipus is curiously transformed; no man *can* be happy until he reaches old age.

Because they had not put themselves in the way to be destroyed by passion, the cloistered virtue of Grannis and Miss Baker enables them to survive and find a few final moments of happiness. Better a muted *telos* than a false one that is doomed to non-fulfillment.[10]

Another potent use of the old person as touchstone occurs when a writer makes an explicit link between the wise, or at least benign, old person and the dying social order which he represents, a motif we observed in mild form in Trollope's *Barchester Towers.* In both Anton Chekhov's *The Cherry Orchard* and Bernard Shaw's *Heartbreak House,* the old man-old order motif becomes not merely a passing lament or fleeting alarm, but a means of throwing a sometimes harsh light on both the emerging new order and the one it is replacing.

At one point in *The Cherry Orchard,* Firs, the eighty-seven-year-old servant, briefly assumes the stance of the wise old prophet who could intuitively grasp omens of impending disaster. Just as "the owl hooted and the samovar hummed" before the emancipation of the serfs (from Fir's point of view, a disaster that was the primal cause of the present social chaos),[11] so now strange sounds arouse anxiety as the family awaits word of the sale of its estate to Lopahin, personification of the new mercantilism.

Through bits of conversation between Firs and the impudent young Yasha, we learn of the breakdown in respect that has come with the new social order. Yet even when Yasha claims he is sick of old Firs and wishes he would drop dead, Firs retains his dignity and indeed his authority. "Ech you . . . silly young cuckoo," he taunts Yasha back, foreshadowing the last line of the play, when he repeats those words after noting the utter hopelessness of his own condition. Though, like the old people in certain Indian and Eskimo societies, Firs passively submits to the reality of his abandonment and impending death, his repetition of his taunt to Yasha rescues the final scene from mere pathos and reinforces his dual role. On the one hand, he is there to embody the play's major theme, the passing of the old order; on the other hand, he manages in a few deft strokes to indict both the irresponsibility of Mme Ranevskaya's generation and the hollowness of those who are now moving into positions of power. The elderly victim is also the only person who can genuinely look before and after, not with the fanaticism of a Trofimov, but with the resigned wisdom of a turn-of-the-century Russian Tiresias.

"Old men are dangerous; it doesn't matter to them what is going to happen to the world," claims the sardonic eighty-eight-year-old Captain Shotover in Shaw's *Heartbreak House*. Like Firs, Shotover frequently reminisces about the good old days, and is taunted for his senility. But the Captain enacts with far more vigor the role of a Janus-like prophet, lamenting both the dangers of the newly emerging managerial ethic and the ivory-tower decadence of the pre-war aristocracy who are allowing the Mangans to take over Britain.

Throughout the play, Shotover's words and actions are marked by irony and ambivalence. He can blithely dismiss demands that he play the wise old man by taking refuge in his dotage. Yet there is no real happiness in yielding to a recognized loss of power and responsibility. "I feel nothing but the accursed happiness I have dreaded all my life long: the happiness that comes as life goes, the happiness of yielding and dreaming instead of resisting and doing, the sweetness of the fruit that is going rotten" (p.130).[12] Despite his protests, however, Shotover can still act and resist. Prominent among his "own little wants and hobbies" is working out plans to literally destroy his fellow-creatures with dynamite. Though he comes on ostensibly as one who would preserve the "ship" of the old order by annihilating the avaricious Mangans, in the end, when Mangan and his cohort are indeed destroyed by a German bomb setting off the dynamite blast, Shotover sardonically laments that thirty pounds of good dynamite have been wasted. Ultimately, he is not merely a tenacious embodiment of dying tradition, but a cynically sagacious perceiver of the truth that mass suicide of the gentile aristocracy, including himself, is more the order of the day than murder of the new pragmatic materialism that has already attained a *de facto* victory (p.25).

Shotover's key roles coalesce in the final dialogue: his cynical resignation to the deserved annihilation of Heartbreak House and his superior perception of reality, despite his dotage. It is through implicit comparison with the silly comments of the other characters that the latter point becomes clear. Shotover is a symbol of England's might in the freebooting morality of nineteenth-century colonialism. As an old man he is caught between two worlds—the world of the aristocracy that his freebooting helped to create, and the usurping managerial class. Surely Shaw does not intend for us to admire Shotoverian piracy, but using an old person as a satiric touchstone can tilt the reader's sympathies toward the old order. When fictively embodied in old age, such reactionary habits of mind are no longer functional and, therefore, no longer threatening; they may even become attractive in comparison with the values of the emerging new order.

III. Old Person as Symptom

Instead of regret for the condition of "the age" as symbolized by the old person, regret for old age itself informs another group of fiction. Unlike those works in which old age is a touchstone for revealing the weaknesses of the younger members of society, works such as Welty's "A Visit of Charity," Chekhov's "Old Age," and Rosalind Wright's novel, *Rocking,* focus on and lament the condition of old age itself—although frequently the lament may also implicate society. Spotlighting the physical, psychological, and social reality of old age could be potentially bathetic, but need not be.

Without giving way to mawkishness, for example, Arnold Bennett in *The Old Wives' Tale* is remarkably sympathetic to the two protagonists, Constance and Sophia Baines, even when the sisters reach the end of their generally banal lives. Constance in particular seems at first to accept her old age cheerfully, despite sciatica and rheumatism and the erosion of the slow-paced, intimate lifestyle of the Bursley she had known all her life. But the impending vote to make Bursley part of a federation of the Five Towns arouses "pain and scornful wrath" in the ailing Constance. The federation movement is accompanied by theatrical hoopla, against the backdrop of the new Midland Clothiers Company. The handbills and colored posters of the latter proclaim the triumph of modern mass-merchandising techniques over the simple ways of the old family store upon whose site the Midland Company now stands. The intensity of regret is heightened when Constance is told to leave the house of her birth so that it may be converted for the convenience of Midland's new manager (another variant on the ancient custom of ostracizing the aged who can no longer contribute to the economic well-being of the community). Though in severe pain, she forces herself out to vote against the federation movement that would totally obliterate the values to which she and her family had dedicated their energies; but the new world of Bursley "could pay small heed to sciatical old ladies confined to sofas and firesides."[13] The exhaustion of voting leads to her final illness, whose pain she accepts stoically; even when she recognizes that death is imminent, she does not indulge in self-pity, but having relieved her anger through the heroic act of voting, accepts her lot "with a sort of tart but not sour cheerfulness" (p.607).

Despite the dignity Constance sustains, the overall tone of the last pages of Bennett's novel is one of regret, regret that a person may live many years only to reach such a resigned insight as "Well, that is what life is!" (p.607). Constance Baines embodies her creator's commitment to realism so thoroughly that she encompasses both its strength—the excision of those magical illusions that would cross over into fairy-tale and myth—and its weakness—the grayness that comes with a sacrifice of even a fleeting hope for some grasp of meaning and grace at life's end.

Tillie Olsen's sixty-nine-year-old Eva in "Tell Me A Riddle," while encompassing some of the same petrifaction of the spirit as Constance Baines, takes on such pathetically heroic strength in her final illness that she becomes a focal point not only for the author's regrets about American society's lack of provision for human fulfillment, but also for the failure of all revolutionary dreams. Refusing both a retreat to the smug substitute world of The Haven, one of those Senior Citizen Communities promising glorious days of craft therapy and reading circles ("*Never again to be forced to move to the rhythms of others*"[14]), and also the conventionally expected submission to the rewards of the grandmother role, Eva cannot quite stifle the claims of that spirited but doomed quest for meaning and action which has haunted her throughout a life of disappointment and self-sacrifice. Yet, despite her urge to drive forward in a search for meaning, the dying Eva eventually does retreat—literally into the closed space of a closet so that she may sheathe herself against the noises of her grandchildren, and psychologically into recollections of her early days of political activism in pogrom-ridden Russia. Her retreat to the past is not sentimentalized, however, and even in her most pained moments Eva can transcend her own condition and cry out about the futility of any human quest for knowledge beyond that grasped by the immediate senses: "The music . . . still it is there and we do not hear; knocks, and our poor human ears too weak. What else, what else we do not hear?" (p.143).

Olsen always presents Eva in context, either with her family or with members of the community, like the jolly geriatrician who claims "Old age is a sickness only if one makes it so." Consequently, we have a particularly vivid picture of the old person as a symptom of far-flung social breakdown, even though the plight of Eva remains the central focus. None of the children can respond adequately to their mother, nor can Eva's husband, who himself comes through as a victim of social conditions, but with a different awareness and less sensitivity than his wife. In the end only grand-daughter Jeannie has the ability to weave some threads of compassion through the torn netting of family relationships in mid-twentieth-century America. Eva's isolation makes a powerful statement about many facets of the modern malaise: the shattering of family ties, the frustrations of the sensitive woman who has never had a chance to fulfill her ambitions, the phoniness of complacent efforts to deny or euphemize old age, and the failure of once fervid revolutionary dreams.

IV. Old Person as Mirror

There are those who, because of their generally negative attitude both toward specific social value systems and also toward the very purposefulness of life itself, find the link between old age and civilization writ large a most auspicious means of expressing their views. To move from symptoms to mirror is to move from a socio-political frame of reference, which even at its most devastating can carry an implicit hope for change, to a philosophical frame of reference, in which there is no fictive need to suggest that "if only such-and-so would occur, things would be better." Life simply is absurd and irrational; human beings are all caught in a trap where reason and progress, at any age, are merely an illusion. In such works human foibles are seen as reflections in microcosm of the irrational nature of a larger absurdity.

Muriel Spark is one of the more genial exponents of this stance, which is always satirical at its core. In *Memento Mori,* one of a very few novels that focuses exclusively on the very old,[15] she places the absurdity in question in the particular social context of upper-class London; but her geriatric troupe could with some minor modifications be acting out its ridiculous schemes in any civilized milieu. Toward the end of her *tour de force,* the sanest character of the lot, Jean Taylor, claims "We all appear to ourselves frustrated in our old age . . . because we cling to everything so much. But in reality we are still fulfilling our lives."[16] But fulfilling and clinging in the end amount to the same thing: the rakish Godfrey Colston still chases skirts at eighty-seven; the obsessive social researcher Alec Warner merely shifts his focus to an obsessive "scientific" cataloguing of all the signs of senility he observes in his peers; the greedy Miss Pettigrew sustains her greed and dishonesty at seventy-three; the old ladies in the Maud Long Medical Ward eagerly respond to the news of their daily horoscopes even though they are totally sealed off from the exciting developments promised by the pseudo-teleology of astrology. Even the repeated, mysterious telephone warning "Remember you must die" does not change the psychic topography of Lettie Colston (or subsequent recipients of the same message), for the need to deny one's own death is a habit of long, long standing.

Lettie is battered to death in a totally irrational crime; the evil Miss Pettigrew gets her legacy because of an absurd tangle of events; eventually everyone dies from one random cause or another. With all of these happenings expressed in the breezy understatement characteristic of drawing room comedy, Spark manages to demolish both human pretensions to significance and any larger hope the reader may sustain about existence as an ordered progress toward some sublime reward. Even precisely described physical decay can be accomodated to such a fiction without becoming either grotesque or mawkish: "As we get older these affairs of the bladder and kidneys do become so important to us. I hope she has a commode by her bedside, you know how difficult it is for old bones to manage a pot" (p.36). Age is all simply a matter of fact.

With its constant parody of sentimental clichés about the rewards of aging and of such allied tropes as the wise old man, indeed, with its parody of the very notion of *telos* itself, Eugene Ionesco's play, *The Chairs,* strikingly exemplifies the narrative suitability of old characters to reinforce the author's anti-Aristotelian, anti-Cartesian vision. "We have our dignity, our self-respect," Ionesco's Old Woman (age ninety-four) protests to one of the invisible "guests" who arrive in the circular room where she and her ninety-five-year-old husband are assembling their imaginary company to await the Orator who will reveal the Old Man's supreme message. But the woman's grotesque erotic gestures, the man's Prufrockian regrets about not having dared enough, and their shared illusions about family relationships (including the imaginary son) demonstrate a shattered consciousness that is anything but dignified.

Neither their past life nor their present charades are truly dynamic. Their pantomime of carrying in chairs for their "guests" begins frenetically, but gradually slows down until both the Old Man and the Old Woman assume static positions by their respective windows, positions they maintain until they throw themselves out the windows at the end of the play.[17] As if the ironic point needs capping, Ionesco has the Old Man claim shortly after the pantomime, "But of course, I believe in progress, uninterrupted progress. . . ."[18] Even the Orator, revealer of the play's mock-*telos,* remains immobile much of the time he is on stage. Rationalistic views of time, language, thought patterns, and purposive human action are reduced to the chaotic ramblings of senility. We are all senile, therefore we are. . . .

At least Ionesco's old couple has some illusions of a *telos.* In Samuel Beckett's *Endgame,* stasis in the form of a meaningless accumulation of moments informs the play's time-consciousness from Clov's opening speech on: "Grain upon grain, one by one, and one day, suddenly there's a heap, a little heap, the impossible heap."[19] All that remains is to end the accumulation, but since even that semblance of purposive action would require a break with the four characters' inertia, the play's action totters uneasily on the threshold between endurance of yet more futile routine and truncated wishes to break, once and for all, the accumulation of static moments;

> HAMM: Enough, it's time it ended, in the shelter, too.
> (Pause)
> And yet I hesitate, I hesitate to. . . .
> to end. Yes, there it is, it's time it ended and
> yet I hesitate to (p.3).

The very form in which Hamm expresses his wish echoes the spastic repetition characteristic of the play's frame of reference. Yet another sort of movement, akin like stasis and repetition to the condition of old age, works contrapuntally throughout the play—dissolution. As Ruby Cohn has noted, things are constantly running out, such as food, pain-killers, bicycle wheels, and ultimately words themselves.[20]

Though only Nagg and Nell, who live like bottled specimens in sheeted ashcans, are blatantly old, one might say that the entire quartet epitomizes the stagnant waiting and sealed "destiny" of old age at its most grotesque extreme: Hamm is blind, crippled, and conscious only of abandonment and loss; Clov's movements consist of meaningless tasks until the final ambiguous moment when he stands at the door dressed for a journey but "impassive and motionless." Once again, we are all old, therefore we are. Though because of their literally discarded condition, Nagg and Nell contribute the greatest shock value, Beckett's fun-house mirror has been constructed to catch the horrified reflections of all who have been unfortunate enough to be born to human consciousness.

V. Conclusions

To move from the celebration of old Phoenix Jackson's stoical journey through the woods to the macabre presentation of Nagg and Nell's incarceration in their ash-cans may seem like a leap across centuries of social and literary responses to old age. Yet the two works that begin and end our overview were written within a bit more than fifteen years of each other, "A Worn Path" in 1941, and *Endgame* in 1957. Neither of these two approaches to old age, or any of the many we have discussed in between, represents in itself, a convention of the modern response. In terms of literature, then, we claim no uniquely modern response to old age, despite the de-mystification of its powers when compared to some earlier societies. Remarkably similar perspectives turn up in widely separated eras—the ridicule and satire in Ionesco and Beckett is foreshadowed by the ridicule of the aged in Roman comedy; Elizabethan drama is filled with the same stereotyped *senex iratus* figures used by Eugene O'Neill and Patrick White; wise old men and women appear in such diverse and historically separated writers as Euripides, Shakespeare, Faulkner, Welty, and Solzhenitsyn.

Indeed, what is distinctively modern may well be the rich diversity with which writers treat old age, a diversity reflecting perhaps our modern cultural pluralism. The only definitive claim one can make is that what might seem on the surface as inimical to narrative development—the bounded, non-teleological condition of old age—has been put to a multiplicity of uses, some of which exploit that condition as an end in itself, and others which invest it with possibilities that reach far beyond the condition's surface limitations. But in each case the condition of old age has a marked effect on the shape of the resultant narration.

Conclusion

CAN OLD BE BEAUTIFUL? OR CREATIVE? REMARKS OF AN OCTOGENARIAN

By Henri Peyre

[Henri Peyre brings to his subject sixty years of experience as a scholar. He makes the point that while literature—lyric poetry in particular—dwells on the problems of adolescence and young adulthood, society has been responding to the demographic trends which since 1800 or so have doubled the life expectancy of those reaching sixty. Politicians and advertisers have begun wooing the old for their votes and dollars; literature has lagged behind.

Peyre takes Shakespeare in particular to task, for depicting old people as having to choose between victimization and renunciation. And with rare exceptions like Sophocles and Goethe, "the old themselves seldom rise to lofty and poetical heights when pondering over their experience and their useless accumulated wisdom." The thinking of the old appears trite and inadequate in mathematics and the sciences, in essays and philosophy. Only by sustained attention to the concrete, as painters, musicians, or political men of action, Peyre believes, can the elderly retain their vigor.

In aid of the moral support of the old, Henri Peyre makes an appeal for an anthology of the great poetry on death. Outside this area, we suffer a shortage of noteworthy literary depictions of old age, Peyre believes. Young writers lack the experience to create rich, convincingly aged characters; old writers like Goethe or Wordsworth in their last years either feel too weighed down by renunciation to depict a fiery, embattled old person, or else they turn nostalgically toward the past. So their most memorable characters are liable not to be genuinely aged ones. Aside from the arbitrary label "one hundred years old," for example, the Faust of Goethe's Part II, Act V has few of the characteristics or limitations of the old person, other than an implied decrease of interest in sex, a near-senile impatience (but impatience always was his greatest fault), and a broadening sense of solidarity as he thinks for the first time of building a future society rather than a private love-nest.

I would argue, however, that the conclusion to be drawn from Henri Peyre's compendium of examples is not that old people seldom create noteworthy depictions of themselves: rather, to seek such depictions exclusively in poetry, fiction, and drama is to restrict one's search to an unpromising place. Each season of human life has its own genres: the outstanding self-portraits of old people are memoirs. Unlike the self-absorbed, self-justifying Rousseauistic confession, and unlike the autobiography with its fascination with one's personal etiology which produces an emphasis upon childhood, the memoir reflects a broad sense of contemplative solidarity in the spirit of which the author integrates his personal destiny into the flow of history and the succession of the generations. The memoir produces literary and psychological masterpieces—Chateaubriand, Winston Churchill, Charles DeGaulle. Few people know these texts: they seldom are read in schools because they are too long. Moreover, the authors' viewpoint on events, at once impassioned and detached, proposes no overt models of behavior to use. Seeking guidance for life, we therefore tend to turn, in reading life stories, to biographies which primarily highlight the individual's achievements, and to works in the tradition of the Augustinian confession, like Montaigne's Essays. *Such literature, like that of late middle age, is oriented still toward generativity, toward guiding the young. It takes us by the hand and insistently proposes models for behavior, in the style of an officious aunt or uncle rather than of an indulgent grandparent—Eds.]*

SOME OF US, and not only superannuated and rancorous critics, have repeatedly, and thus far vainly, deplored the paucity of subjects around which men of letters, poets in particular, have woven their wreaths of eulogy, complaint, self-pity and mourning. Love, youth, and war have made up their staple nourishment for twenty-five hundred years.

Meanwhile, the span of years during which a person of sixty may reasonably expect to survive has doubled or trebled since 1800 or so. Old people may constitute a drain on social security funds and hospitals; still they are courted by politicians, department stores, movie houses, television advertisers. The "little old lady," as she is patronizingly alluded to, is sought after by savings institutions, stockbrokers, tourist agencies, and car salesmen. Men of sixty-eight are seen jauntily jogging along our roads. They even manage to eliminate from the highest and most demanding offices rivals two decades younger. In China, Russia, and Iran a gerontocracy tenaciously clings to power.

Still literature and the arts prefer to ignore senior citizens. In several languages, the term corresponding to the Latin "senectus," to the French "vieillesse," to the Spanish "vejez" is prudishly eschewed. Worse yet, generations of school boys were made to recite, and scoff at, the spirited enumeration of the last stages of life given by melancholy Jaques in *As You Like It:* he mocks the final among those stages as but "second childishness and mere oblivion/Sans teeth, sans eyes, sans taste, sans everything." The wretched old men might just as well fade away. The gallery of Shakespearean old fools, from Shylock to Polonius, mad Lear and the royal dotards of *Cymbeline* and *A Winter's Tale,* is a pathetic or ludicrous one. Prospero himself, tired of arousing the elements and of chastising the plotters around him, has little left to look forward to, once his daugther is married; he will retire in Milan and wait for his own demise: "Every third thought shall be my grave."

Wordsworth died in 1850, at eighty, having outlived poets twenty-five years his junior. The "lost leader" had by then ceased fighting for progressive causes; he cared little to depict the blessings of old age. His most memorable lines remain those in which he reminisced on his enjoyment of "strange fits of passion" and the nascent revolution in France when "to be young was very heaven." The towering giant among the writers astride the eighteenth and the nineteenth centuries, and the one who is credited with the most Olympian serenity, Goethe, had reached his seventy-fourth year when a nineteen-year-old girl inspired him with his most touching elegy. He had been tactfully rejected when he proposed to her family. Still he insisted on believing that "the serene peace of love in the presence of the beloved" might have fallen to him as the reward of his long years of joy and of sorrow. He yielded sorrowfully to that resignation which he had often counseled to others, but not practiced easily. He alluded in the Marienbad elegy to his "endless tears." He felt torn asunder by the duel of life and death in him, experiencing again the conflict of two souls in his breast to which Faust had alluded. His last love elegy counts among the most tragic poems of desire and regret left by an aging man. Valiantly, Goethe recovered; he completed the second part of *Faust;* he confided his reflections of an octogenarian to Eckermann, then died at eighty-two after that last and pathetic ascent to demonic heights.

In Britain, another advocate of restraint and resignation, Matthew Arnold, had sternly advised his countrymen to close their Byron and go to school with Goethe. He dreamt of Sophocles by the Aegean sea, on the beach at Dover. He aspired after a clear-sighted and constructive pessimism. But his poems on aging men fall far short of the Greek tragedian and of Goethe. "Consolation" is facile and does not rise above a prosaic admonition. "In utrumque paratus" proves hardly worthy of the proud stoic resolution implicit in the title. The lines in which he describes aging hardly ennoble that inevitable experience. "What is it to grow old?" he asks in "Growing old." His answer holds out scant encouragement. It is to pine childishly for the days of youth, for the heart that once stirred, to retain "dull remembrance of a change,/But no emotion—none." Then the old end up as the phantoms of what they once had been. Elsewhere, without any illusion, Arnold had, pitifully, mourned the sluggishness of mind and body of the aged.

"The heart less bounding at emotion new,/And hope, once crushed, less quick to spring again."

The Irishman Yeats was far remote in his inspiration, imagery and sensitiveness, from Arnold's high seriousness. He proposed no message of intellectual growth or of smiling submission to eternal laws to Britain or to John Bull's other island. He attempted strenuously to delay the onslaught of old age and the ending of one's loving impulses and dreams. In haunting lines, he likened the aged man to "a tattered coat upon a stick," when he was sailing, symbolically, to the country of venerable sages, Byzantium. He evinced no compassion for those who consent to turn into "paltry things" and to forsake the thrills of loving. A year earlier, in 1926, in "The Tower," Yeats, then nearing sixty, exulted with naive pride at feeling younger and bolder than he had been in his prime. What a revolting plight to be saddled with an accumulation of years, "this absurdity . . . This caricature / Decrepit age that has been tied to me / As to a dog's tail."

A poet vastly different from Yeats, more immune to the temptations and the pitfalls of passion, T. S. Eliot, was even more sarcastic in his warnings against the spurious wisdom (in truth mere folly) of old men: their cowardly fear of belonging to others or to God, their disregard of the one true wisdom, that of humility ("East Coker"). Earlier, in a spirited meditative monologue first intended for *The Waste Land,* "Gerontion," the self-incriminating old man had blandly introduced himself thus: "I am an old man / A dull head among windy spaces / . . . An old man in a draughty house / Under a windy knob." Passion has deserted him and what need would he have of it? Again, in "Little Gidding" Eliot returned to that favorite theme of his: the stern indictment of the preposterous illusions of the old. Fourteen lines, beginning with "Let me disclose the gifts reserved for age" number among the most unsparing in literature in their denunciation of the venomous rage, the idle regrets, the self-deceit of those whose "body and soul begin to fall asunder." Charity has deserted the Anglo-Catholic poet when he caricatures those most hollow of men, those who have survived sixty.

One may read impatience, resentment at the aged persons,

and fear of soon resembling them in the bitter portrayals of those who no longer know how to provide models for the young. The old themselves seldom rise to lofty poetical heights when pondering over their experience and their useless accumulated wisdom.

If the praise of old age seldom inspired poets, it has even more seldom extracted very great treatises from philosophers and essayists. Cicero's *De Senectute* ranks among the most perfunctory of his works. He drew up that shallow dialogue during retirement, between two periods of banishment brought about by his busy and ill-starred political action. He presented Cato the Elder, who had died in the previous century (the second B.C.) as the ideal old man, accepting the decline of accumulated years with fortitude. Cato (or Cicero) draws from Greek history and literature the traditional models of revered sages: Nestor and Laertes in Homeric epics, Solon as the exemplary statesman, Pythagoras, Plato and a cluster of other philosophers, the polished orator Isocrates who wrote his last discourses at 94, and Gorgias the sophist who, it is reported, still composed orations while a centenarian.

To those who, in old age, mourn the waning of physical vigor, Cicero offers the joys of conversation as a substitute. The comfort, however, may strike us as a feeble one. It is a complaint of old people that they find few persons of their age left to converse with, or to listen to, and the younger ones evince scant interest in their yarns. Penning elaborate letters, as Cicero generously did, and moralizing treatises, might prove a less frustrating pastime, since the septuagenarian does not have to wait for an answer, or for a yawn. Cicero himself failed to live long enough to put his tepid precepts into practice. At sixty-three, he suffered a gruesome, barbaric death at the hands of the partisans of Anthony, against whom he had sided.

Twenty centuries later, some inveterate moralists have undertaken to tender the lessons of their long experience to the younger generations. It was in part, with them, an attempt to remind the audience which had praised them in the past that they were still alive, and worth listening to. They also drew argument from the precedents of other creators in the past who had produced significant works after seventy-five.

Henry Miller, who had never coveted serenity or even profundity, composed after eighty and left behind for a listless posterity a rather shallow piece, "On Turning Eighty" (Sextet, 1980). V. S. Pritchett, after reaching eighty, dealt with a similar theme with more detachment in the *New York Times Sunday Magazine* section of December 14, 1980. Another writer born with the century, Malcolm Cowley, the chronicler of the "lost generation" of exiles of the nineteen-twenties, expanded an article from *Life Magazine* into a short volume: *The View From Eighty* (The Viking Press, 1980). With gentle humor and sanity, Cowley derived some pride from listing the writers of past centuries who had retained mental vigor and even imaginative freshness long past sixty. He spurned the suggestion that a last identity crisis necessarily befalls octogenarians. Gloating over the obituaries of persons younger than themselves in the daily press encourages aging survivors in their refusal to surrender. In Britain, John Cowper Powys (1872–1963) proved hardly more original in his reflections on old age. The sermonizing proffered to the unquiet senior citizens by theologians is hardly more comforting. A Roman Catholic moralist, J. M. Nouwen, in *Aging* (Doubleday, 1974), volunteered advice, in rather vapid prose, to those who feel disturbed by the increasingly larger number of old people in our midst. Let all of us receive light from them, he advises, "Aging . . . can be understood, affirmed and experienced as a process of growth by which the mystery of life is slowly revealed to us." But have many octogenarians truly gained a deeper awareness of the mysteries of life or of death?

Plato, in the *Gorgias* and in the *Phaedo,* had offered the pursuit of death as the true goal for him who devotes himself to philosophy. It is questionable if such meditation ever proved very illuminating either among the ancient thinkers or among the Christian ones. Montaigne and Rousseau had pondered over the end of Socrates longer than on the death of Christ. They could hope that they might imitate the former, or offer Socrates as a model that laymen would follow. Yet there is not a little intoxication with words and a fair dose of complacency with the lengthy tirades which Plato lends to the master in his prison, invoking the melodious singing of the dying swan and delivering his message of faith in immortality. Socrates was then seventy, and that venerable age would probably correspond to eighty-five in our century when the life expectancy has lengthened. He must have realized that his condemnation merely enabled him to anticipate the verdict of nature by a few years and to earn a martyr's fame. Perhaps he is made to confide more sincerely, if more prosaically, in Xenophon's pedestrian *Memorabilia* (Part iv, ch. viii, 8) where he deems his end preferable to a burdensome old age: "If I am to live on, I shall perhaps be forced to pay the old man's tribute: to become blind and deaf and dull of wit, quicker at forgetting. . . . Misery and bitterness would certainly be my lot."

The serenity of such resilient and, one might think, passionless septuagenarians is probably a myth. A few, a very few, who had chosen to live a prudent existence, sheltered from emotional crises, may like Fontenelle, reach their hundredth year with little more than "a certain difficulty in being." But there are others who had liberally engaged in fights, controversies, vituperations and evinced, after seventy, little taste for relenting or for repenting. Voltaire was one of these. So was Walter Savage Landor in Britain (1775–1864), who outlived several political and literary upheavals. His *Heroic Idylls* appeared when he was eighty-eight. Few epitaphs are as famous, and as mendacious, as the one that he penned for himself, proudly beginning: "I strove with none, for none was worth my strife."

The writers of antiquity may have been endowed with a more resistant constitution than that of the moderns. Plato thought little of the old as useful citizens in a republic. Still, he was over seventy when he composed the Timaeus and the Laws. He must have died at eighty. Isocrates was apparently close to one hundred when, in eloquent and flowing orations, he sang the praise of Athens and attempted to convince all the Hellenes to unite. The Oresteia apparently dates from the last decade of Aeschylus' long life. Sophocles completed his Philoctetes at eighty-seven, his Oedipus Coloneus even later, and he was then accused by ungrateful children of being in dotage. He had reached ninety when he died.

It seems to some a paradox that men of action (generals,

statesmen, bankers occasionally) often survive to an advanced age. Incessant political fights, greed, lust for power and the conviction that none of their juniors are qualified to replace them, probably keep them alive, energetic and domineering. Churchill, Adenauer, De Gaulle astonished and at times angered their younger contemporaries. Clemenceau was seventy-six when, in 1917, he assumed power in France. He displayed fierce energy as a war leader. He incurred the annoyance and met with the grudging respect of allied statesmen while they were drafting the Treaty of Versailles in 1919. In the past, there had been no dearth of combative old leaders, reluctant to yield power: Louis XIV in France, Franz Josef of Austria. Pope Innocent III had reached a venerable age when, in 1204, he incited the warriors of the Fourth Crusade to sack Constantinople. Another Italian, laden with even more years, the Venetian Doge Enrico Dandolo, at eighty-four, captured the Adriatic city of Zara, plundered it ruthlessly, then directed his combative rage to the treasures of Constantinople and appropriated the horses "of St. Mark" for his native city.

Yet and despite exceptions, it must be acknowledged that, in mathematics and physics in particular, boldness in offering new hypotheses, insolence in challenging prevailing views and methods, and imaginative originality have seldom been the mark of men over forty. The second half of Einstein's career pales beside his earlier achievement. Newton, who died at eighty-five, wasted the last decades of his life in unprofitable and singularly unscientific pursuits. It has become a common practice, and probably a well-meant one, in many western countries to withdraw scientists from their laboratories and research institutes after the middle of their lives. They then become respected and harmless academicians or administrators of foundations, where it may be hoped they will not stand in the way of the irreverent discoveries of their pupils. Countries which had once boasted of being revolutionary, in Eastern Europe and in Asia, have frequently become those which cling to the past most stubbornly: few "juniors" not yet sixty-five gain membership in their venerable academies or their honored "praesidia."

For reasons which would deserve exploring, orchestra conductors (Toscanini, Monteaux, Stokowski and a score of others) and virtuoso performers (Casals, Rubinstein) appear to retain their sway upon their audiences the longest. It has been hinted that, as may be the case for the members of the French Academy, their awareness of the impatience of their younger rivals, praying for their demise and waiting to inherit their seat or their baton, helps them survive. It is striking that Monteverdi (1567–1643), J. Sebastian Bach (1685–1750), Handel (1685–1759), Haydn (1732–1809), even hardly serene Berlioz (1803–1869) and Verdi (1813–1901) went on producing great works late in their careers. Yet they had not spared efforts or shunned battles.

Painters do not have to meet the challenge of the public headlong. The early decades of their productive lives had often been spent in obscurity and poverty. Rewards seldom honor them before they have at last succeeded in imposing their standards by which they will be judged. They refuse to feel weary after those long years of uphill fight. Giovanni Bellini painted admirable portraits a little before he died, at eighty-seven. Tintoretto lived on until seventy-six. Titian did some of his most famous canvases, such as "The Battle of Lepanto" at the ripe age of ninety-five. At ninety-seven he declared that he was just beginning to understand what the art of painting was all about. He was almost a centenarian when he died in 1576. Hokusai died at eighty-nine, in 1849; he signed the engravings which later won the praise of Whistler and Manet: "Hokusai, the old man mad about drawing." He was almost on his death-bed when he uttered one regret: "If heaven were to grant me but five more years, I might become a truly great artist. . . . At ninety, I might penetrate into the mystery of things." Goya was eighty-two when, in 1828, deaf and sick, in his exile at Bordeaux, he still accomplished some of his most robust work. Ingres, the most bellicose of academicians, died in 1867 at eighty-seven, having just completed some of his most youthful canvases. Monet in his eighties had lost none of his freshness and energy as a painter. He died at eighty-six. Degas, perhaps kept alive by the sarcastic temper which was his and by his desire to outdo all young rivals, kept on producing to his eighty-third year. Matisse lived for eighty-five years and, struggling with ill-health, did the frescoes of the Chapel of the Rosary, at Vence, not long before his death in 1954. Picasso's fecundity did not flag until his ninety-first year; his haughty disregard for younger artists persisted until then, as did his superstitious terror of death. He would have fulminated like a wrathful god at those who dared advise him to rest.

Does the prospect that creativity need not be extinguished in septuagenarians afford us a more cheerful old age? Does it arm us more securely against the fear of death? Do they suffer from feeling almost eliminated from literature (fictional and dramatic), though less drastically from painting? One of the scarce novels staging with sympathy and gentleness an aged person is that of an English woman of some note, Victoria Sackville West (1892–1962). The title, *All Passion Spent,* was taken from the last words of Milton's epic drama on Samson. The widow of a lord, a former Viceroy of India, whom her late husband had always treated like a pleasant but negligible ornament, comes into her own after he dies. She disregards the counsel of her grown children, who take her to be an incapable old woman. She is visited by a respectful old bachelor, who once had dreamt of arousing her interest. He enjoys her company, then dies and, to her surprise, bequeaths to her a fortune that he had made through investing in art works. To her heirs' dismay, the old lady, by then having learned how to survive in independence, and served by a protective French maid, decides to leave her fortune to the nation. The story is told with humor and reveals a keen insight into the whims and ironical wisdom of an aged person.

Not many aged persons can be foolhardy enough to imagine that they could rival the fecundity of exceptionally gifted artists such as were mentioned above. One of the healthiest marks of courage in America and perhaps elsewhere, in the last decades of the century, is our growing impatience with the hypocrisy and the euphemisms surrounding dying. We are proud of having torn many of the veils with which our predecessors—romantic, Victorian, Preraphaelite—thought they could adorn and soften the stark reality of Eros. But we cling to superstitions and myths where Thanatos is concerned. The mendacious epitaphs, the pretentious monstrosities of funeral monuments in Christian cemeteries, the platitudinous orations uttered around caskets and the ludicrous solemnity of funeral parlors are one of the shames of modern civilization. They account in part for the reluctance of old people to face the inevitable prospect confronting them, with a minimum of dignity.

It has become the fashion at wedding ceremonies to replace, or to supplement, the commonplaces of earlier times on eternal fidelity, obedience of the bride and promises of protection by the bridegroom, with the reading of lines from a love sonnet of old or from a grandiose epithalamion. The poetry on and around death is far richer, more varied, and it rises to even greater heights. An anthology of such poetry, through the sheer power and intensity of its best texts, would be more exalting than the many and often depressingly wearisome anthologies of erotic verse or prose. Elegies in Greek and Latin, Milton's *Lycidas,* Shelley's *Adonais,* wreaths woven by poets over the tombs of Baudelaire or Théophile Gautier, laments upon the deaths of Irish revolutionaries, of toreros, of soldiers, by Yeats, Lorca, or Russian or English poets make up one of the most original achievements of world poetry. Read or reread by aging persons, they would afford a more aesthetic and ennobling comfort than perfunctory clichés about the immortality of the soul and the resurrection of the body. The systematic uglifying of death appears to some of us as one of the blights of our civilization. The old should rise up to the challenge of society in our time and, with more pride in their past achievement if they happen to have been "creative," to listen, and to respond, with greater dignity, to the "immortal longings" in themselves.

NOTES

Introduction

1. Walter G. Moss, *Humanistic Perspectives on Aging: An Annotated Bibliography and Essay* (Ann Arbor: Institute of Gerontology, The University of Michigan-Wayne State University, 1976).

2. Richard Freedman, "Sufficiently Decayed: Gerontophobia in English Literature," in Stuart F. Spicker, Kathleen M. Woodward, and David D. Van Tassel, eds., *Aging and the Elderly: Humanistic Perspectives in Gerontology* (Atlantic Highlands, New Jersey: Humanities Press, Inc., 1978), p. 49.

3. Robert N. Butler, "The Life Review: An Interpretation of Reminiscence in the Aged," *Psychiatry,* 26 (1963): 65–76.

4. Frederick Wyatt, "Psychology and the Humanities: A Case of No-Relationship," in James F. T. Bugenthal, ed., *Challenges of Humanistic Psychology* (New York: McGraw-Hill, 1967), pp. 296–300.

5. Sigmund Freud, *On Creativity and the Unconscious* (New York: Harper & Row, 1958), p. 45.

6. Erik H. Erikson, *Identity and the Life Cycle: Selected Papers* (New York: W. W. Norton, 1980), especially Chapter Two, "Growth and Crises of the Healthy Personality." This volume was originally published as the first number of *Psychological Issues,* 1959.

7. Erik H. Erikson, "The Problem of Ego Identity," in Maurice R. Stein, Arthur J. Vidich, and David Manning White, eds., *Identity and Anxiety: Survival of the Person in Mass Society* (New York: Free Press, 1960), p. 51.

8. See Erikson, *Identity and the Life Cycle;* Grace Ganter and Margaret Yeakel, *Human Behavior and the Social Environment: A Perspective for Social Work Practice* (New York: Columbia University Press, 1980), pp. 133–136; and A. Bandura, *Social Learning Theory* (Englewood Cliffs, New Jersey: Prentice-Hall, 1977), pp. 2–13, 29–34.

9. Carola H. Mann, "Mid-Life and the Family: Strains, Challenges, and Options of the Middle Years," in William H. Norman and Thomas J. Scaramella, eds., *Mid-Life* (New York: Brunner-Mazel, 1980), p. 144.

10. See Lillian Troll, Sheila Miller, and Robert Atchley, *Families in Later Life* (Belmont, California: Wadsworth Publishing Co., 1979).

11. I. A. Richards, "The Future of the Humanities in General Education," in Stein et al. (note 7), p. 388.

12. Kenneth Koch, *I Never Told Anybody: Teaching Poetry Writing in a Nursing Home* (New York: Random House, 1977), p. 95.

13. See Robert N. Butler, "Age-ism: Another Form of Bigotry," *Gerontologist,* 9 (1969): 243–246; Thomas W. Elwood, "Old Age and the Quality of Life," in Martin Bloom, ed., *Life Span Development* (New York: Macmillan, 1980), p. 364; Dorothy Strauss, "Aging and Old Age," in Richard C. Simons and Herbert Pardes, eds., *Understanding Human Behavior in Health and Illness* (Baltimore: Williams and Wilkins, 1977), p. 371; Eric Pfeiffer, Chapter One in Ewald Busse and Eric Pfeiffer, *Mental Illness in Later Life* (Washington, D.C.: American Psychiatric Association, 1973); M. Powell Lawton and Leonard Gottesman, "Psychosocial Services to the Elderly," *American Psychologist,* Sept. 1974, p. 690; Marie L. Blank, "Ageism in Gerontologyland," *Journal of Gerontological Social Work,* 2, i (1979): 7–8.

14. Irene Burnside et al., *The Psychosocial Needs of the Aged: Selected Papers* (Los Angeles: Ethel Percy Andrus Gerontology Center, 1977), p. 17; see also the Winter 1979 special issue of the *Journal of Drug Issues.*
15. See Busse (note 13), p. 104.
16. John J. Herr and John H. Weakland, *Counseling Elders and Their Families: Practical Techniques for Applied Gerontology* (New York: Springer Publications, 1979).
17. Arnold van Gennep, *The Rites of Passage,* tr. by Monika B. Vizedom and Gabrielle L. Caffee (Chicago: The University of Chicago Press, 1960), p. 145.
18. Peter N. Stearns, *Old Age in European Society: The Case of France* (New York: Holmes and Meier, 1976), p. 9.
19. See Sula Benet's fascinating case study in cultural anthropology, *Abkhasians: The Long-Living People of the Caucasus* (New York: Holt, Rinehart and Winston, 1974).
20. Cited in E. R. Hughes, ed., *Chinese Philosophy in Classical Times,* Ch. 33 (New York: Gordon, 1977).
21. Claude Lévi-Strauss, *Tristes Tropiques,* tr. John and Doreen Weightman (New York: Atheneum, 1974), p. 287.
22. Nikki Giovanni, "Age," in *Cotton Candy on a Rainy Day* (New York: Morrow Quill Paperbacks, 1980), pp. 44–46.

Editor's Introduction for Chapter 1

1. Reay Tannahill, *Sex in History* (New York: Stein and Day, 1980), pp. 160–161.
2. Peter Stearns, *Old Age in European Society: The Case of France* (New York: Holmes and Meier, 1976), p. 31. We shall again encounter the notion that vital forces are depleted through exertion in Eugene Gray's study of Balzac.
3. Cited in Stearns, pp. 33–34.
4. The best such work I know of is by Robert N. Butler and Myrna I. Lewis, *Love and Sex after Sixty: A Guide for Men and Women in Their Later Years* (New York: Harper and Row, 1976).

Chapter I

1. Félix Lecoy, ed., *Le Roman de la Rose,* Classiques Français du Moyen Age (Paris: Champion, 1965), t. I, ll. 339, 343–51. Translations mine, here and below.
2. Josiah Cox Russell, *Late Ancient and Medieval Population,* Transactions of the American Philosophical Society, New Series, Vol. 48, part 3 (Philadelphia: American Philosophical Society, 1958), pp. 30–3, and *British Medieval Population* (Albuquerque: University of New Mexico Press, 1948), pp. 173–93.

Although there doubtless was a significant difference in living conditions between nobles and peasants, especially in the areas of work, sanitation, and nutrition, it is difficult to agree with the assertion made by Simone de Beauvoir that for peasants in the thirteenth century 30 was "déjà un grand âge" (*La Vieillesse* [The Coming of Age], Paris: Gallimard, 1970, p. 148).

The passage describing the fountain of youth which she cites as evidence is given a more plausible interpretation by Marie-Thérèse Lorcin, who suggests rather that age 30 was considered "l'âge idéal," the typical result of rejuvenation obtained through magical fountains, fruits, stones, and so forth (*Façons de sentir et de penser: les fabliaux français*, Paris: Champion, 1979, p. 95, n. 3).

3. Russell, *British Medieval Population*, tables 8.3–8.11, pp. 180–86.

4. David Herlihy, "Women in Medieval Society," in *The Social History of Italy and Western Europe, 700–1500: Collected Studies* (London: Variorum Reprints, 1978), IX, pp. 6–7, and "Vieillir à Florence au Quattrocento," *Annales: Economies, Sociétés, Civilisations* 24 (1969), p. 1351.

5. In addition to the authority of the Bible, there was the weight of Plato, who died at the 'perfect' age of 81 (the square of 9): Seneca, *Ad Lucilium Epistulae Morales*, 58:31, and Censorinus, *De Die Natali*, 14.

6. Marcel de Fréville, ed., *Les Quatre Ages de l'homme: Traité moral de Philippe de Navarre* (Paris: Firmin Didot, 1888), 194, p. 105.

7. Giovanni Busnelli and Giuseppe Vandelli, eds., *Il Convivio* (Florence: Le Monnier, 1964), IV, 24:6, Vol. II, pp. 310–1.

8. Philippe Ariès, *L'Enfant et la vie familiale sous l'Ancien Régime*, trans. Robert Baldick, *Centuries of Childhood: A Social History of Family Life* (New York: Knopf, 1962), pp. 18–9, 23. Although it is difficult for us, as Ariès points out, to appreciate the importance of this concept of the ages, we may assume that it was not unlike the importance attributed by many people in our more enlightened times to the signs of the zodiac, each with its particular temperament, affinities, and behavior.

Among numerous studies of the divisions of life, see especially Samuel Claggett Chew, *The Pilgrimage of Life* (New Haven: Yale University Press, 1962), and Paul Archambault, "The Ages of Man and the Ages of the World: A Study of Two Traditions," *Revue des Etudes Augustiniennes*, 12 (1966): 193–228.

9. *De Civitate Dei*, ed. B. Dombar (Leipzig: Tubner, 1877), 22:15; Trans. Henry Bettenson, *Concerning the City of God*, ed. David Knowles (Harmondsworth: Penguin, 1972), p. 1056.

10. *Il Convivio* (N 7), IV, 23:1–11, Vol. II, pp. 287–98. In a very ambitious and generally worthwhile study, Maria Schnee Haynes claims that "the greatest number of writers (in the Middle Ages) seem to have considered the age of fifty as the beginning of old age." But she also cites five sources as evidence of "a conspicuous reiteration of the opinion that old age or man's decay begins at the age of forty or soon thereafter." ("The Concept of Old Age in the Late Middle Ages, with Special Reference to Chaucer," Diss. UCLA 1956, pp. 262–3.)

11. See Horace, *Ars Poetica*, ll. 175–6.

12. Some systems associate phlegm with childhood rather than with old age; when the various systems simplify, this association tends to reinforce the idea of a second childhood, with the end of life resembling the beginning.

13. Raymond Klibansky, Erwin Panofsky, and Fritz Saxl, *Saturn and Melancholy: Studies in the History of Natural Philosophy, Religion, and Art* (New York: Basic Books, 1964), especially pp. 159–95. Among medieval assessments of this influence: Alain de Lille, *Anticlaudianus* IV, 8; Jean Froissart, *Le Joli Buisson de Jonece*, ll. 1688–1707; John Gower, *Confessio*

Amantis VII, ll. 935–46; and Chaucer, "The Knight's Tale," ll. 2443–78.

14. Other examples of warriors of epic age may be found in Adolphe Jacques Dickman, *Le Rôle du Surnaturel dans les chansons de geste* (Iowa City: State University of Iowa, 1925), pp. 169–70.

15. Philippa Tristram, *Figures of Life and Death in Medieval English Literature* (London: Paul Elek, 1976), pp. 77–8.

16. Support for this contrast in behavioral expectations was to be found in folk wisdom as well, in the proverb (understandably criticized by many writers), "Young saint, old devil." See J. A. Burrow, " 'Young Saint, Old Devil': Reflections on a Medieval Proverb," *The Review of English Studies,* New Series 30:117 (1979), pp. 385–96.

17. See Erich Kohler, "Sens et fonction du terme 'jeunesse' dans la poésie des troubadours," in *Mélanges offerts à René Crozet,* eds. Pierre Gallais and Yves-Jean Riou (Poitiers: Société d'Etudes Médiévales, 1966), Vol. I, pp. 569–83.

18. *Le Grand Testament Villon,* eds. Rika van Deyck and Romana Zwaenpoel, *François Villon: Oeuvres d' après le manuscrit Coislin* (Saint-Aquilin-de-Pacy (Eure): Mallier, 1974), Tome I, 48, ll. 461–3, p. 66; Brian Woledge, trans., *The Penguin Book of French Verse,* I: *To the Fifteenth Century* (Harmondsworth: Penguin, 1966), p. 319.

19. *Confessio Amantis,* ed. G. C. Macaulay, *The Complete Works of John Gower* (Oxford: Clarendon Press, 1901; rpt. Grosse Pointe, Michigan: Scholarly Press, 1968), Vol. III, Book VIII, ll. 2401–4.

20. Gaston Paris, ed., *Chansons du XVe siècle,* Société des Anciens Textes Français (Paris: Firmin Didot, 1875), CXXI, p. 122. Eustache Deschamps, *Oeuvres complètes* (Paris: Didot, 1878–1903), 1203 VI: 190–1.

21. Deschamps, *Oeuvres,* 463 III:280.

22. Deschamps, *Oeuvres,* 1185 VI:140.

23. G. C. Robinson, ed., *The Works of Geoffrey Chaucer* (Cambridge, Massachusetts: Riverside Press, 1957), "The Merchant's Tale," ll. 1416–22. The manuscripts offer variants for the 'ideal age limit' (p. 1009).

24. *Les Enseignements d' Anne de France à sa fille Susanne de Bourbon,* ed., A.-M. Chazaud (Moulins: Desrosiers, 1878), pp. 107–8; cited by Mathilde Laigle, *Le Livre des Trois Vertus de Christine de Pisan et son milieu historique et littéraire* (Paris: Champion, 1912), p. 352.

25. Axel Wallensköld, ed., *Chansons de Conon de Béthune* (Helsinki: Imprimerie Centrale, 1891), X, pp. 239–43.

26. Marcel Schwob, ed., *Le Parnasse satyrique du XVe siècle: Anthologie de pièces libres* (Paris: Welter, 1905; rpt. Geneva: Slatkine Reprints, 1969), 81, p. 163. Another such situation is depicted in poem 22 of this collection, p. 78.

27. *Ars Poetica,* ll. 156–7, 169, 175–6, 178; Edward Henry Blakeney, trans., and Casper J. Kraemer, Jr., ed., *The Complete Works of Horace* (New York: Modern Library, 1936). The influence of this passage from the *Ars Poetica* is the subject of the study by George R. Coffman, "Old Age from Horace to Chaucer: Some Literary Affinities and Adventures of an Idea," *Speculum,* 9 (1934): 249–77.

28. Satire X, ll. 196, 198; Rolfe Humphries, trans., *The Satires of Juvenal* (Bloomington: Indiana University Press, 1958).

29. *The "Art" of Rhetoric,* trans. John Henry Freese, Loeb Classical Li-

brary (New York: Putnam's Sons, 1926), II. 13.1, pp. 250–1. Aristotle suggests that youth extends to age 30 or 35 and the prime of life to around 49 (II.14.4).

30. Horace in *Odes* IV, 13, and Epode 8, and Juvenal in Satire X, ll. 188–209, to mention only three examples.

31. "Debemus cunctis proponere" (incipit), described and transcribed by Charles Fierville, in *Notices et Extraits des manuscrits de la Bibliothèque Nationale et autres bibliothèques* (Paris: Imprimerie Nationale, 1884), Tome 31, 1ère partie, pp.132–5.

32. Edmond Faral, ed., *Les Arts poétiques du XIIe et du XIIIe siècles.* p.218, ll. 674–8, 680–1, 683–6.

33. Richard Webster, ed., *The Elegies of Maximianus* (Princeton: Princeton University Press, 1900), p. 32, l. 209.

34. See *Cambridge Middle English Lyrics,* ed. Henry A. Person (Seattle: University of Washington Press, 1953), pp. 19–21, and *English Lyrics of the XIIIth Century,* ed. Carleton Brown (Oxford: Clarendon Press, 1932), p. 130.

35. See Coffman, op. cit. (N 27), pp. 254–8.

36. Kenneth McKenzie, "Antonio Pucci on Old Age," *Speculum,* 15 (1940): 160–85, ll. 1–2.

37. Deschamps, *Oeuvres,* 1266 VIII:3–4.

38. "Après jeunesse qui ne meurt devient vieulx." *Recueil de poésies françoises des XVe et XVIe siècles,* ed. Anatole de Montaiglon (Paris: Jannet, 1857), VII, p. 216.

39. Octavien de Saint-Gelais, *Le Séjour d'Honneur,* ed. Joseph Alston James, North Carolina Studies in the Romance Languages and Literatures, 181 (Chapel Hill: University of North Carolina, 1977), ll. 8151–7.

40. *Confessio Amantis,* Book VIII, ll. 2367–71, 2398–404, 2442–6.

41. Ibid., Book VIII, ll. 2773–79.

42. Ibid., Book VIII, ll. 2824–33.

43. The extent to which we may identify Gower the lover with Gower the poet is open to question.

44. Ibid., Book VIII, iii, 5 (Vol. III, p. 450), and ll. 2842–57. The comparison of life to the calendar was popular in the later Middle Ages.

45. *Republic,* I, 329; *De Senectute,* especially XII, 39 and 42 and XIV, 47, where Sophocles is quoted; *Ad Lucilium Epistulae Morales,* 12 and 68: 13–14.

46. *The Poems and Fables of Robert Henryson,* ed. H. Harvey Wood (London: Oliver and Boyd, 1933), pp. 185–86.

47. "D'Aristote et d'Alixandre," ed. T. B. W. Reid, *Twelve Fabliaux* (Manchester, England: Manchester University Press, 1968), pp. 78, 81. See also Chaucer's "Reeve's Tale."

48. Alfonso Martínez de Toledo, *Arcipreste de Talavera, o Corbacho,* ed. Joaquin Gonzales Muela (Madrid: Castalia, 1970), p. 200.

49. *Les Quatre Ages,* 173, p. 95.

50. *Les Lamentations,* II, ll. 3363–6, 3375–8; the corresponding passage in the *Liber Lamentationum Matheoluli* is ll. 2107–12.

51. Lesley Byrd Simpson, trans., *Little Sermons on Sin: The Archpriest of Talavera* (Berkeley: University of California Press, 1959), pp. 194–5.

52. *Les Quatre Ages,* 173–4, pp. 95–6.

53. Ibid., 186, 162–3, pp. 101, 89–90.

54. "Richeut, Old French Poem of the Twelfth Century," ed. Irville C. Lecompte, *Romanic Review* (1913), pp. 261–305; Richard de Fournival, *Pseudo-Ovidius De Vetula: Untersuchungen und Text,* ed. Paul Klopsch (Leiden: Brill, 1967); "De la Viellette ou de la Vieille Truande," *Recueil général et complet des fabliaux des XIIIe et XIVe siècles,* eds., Anatole de Montaiglon and Gaston Raynaud (Paris: Librairie des Bibliophiles, 1883), V:129, pp. 171–8; Boccaccio, *Il Corbaccio.* Matthews mentions others in his excellent article, "The Wife of Bath."

55. An interesting study is Jacques Bailbé, "Le Thème de la vieille femme dans la poésie satirique du XVIe et du début du XVIIe siècles," *Bibliothèque d'Humanisme et Renaissance*, 26 (1964) pp. 98–119. Since medieval society and its literature were male-dominated, men are represented with much more realism, or at least more dimension, than are women. Depictions of women tend to polarize around either the ideal virtue of Mary, as a passive object of idolatry, or the sexually active source of sin, Eve. What we find written about older women generally expresses not only the reality of aging but the aging of an ideal, the nightmare mirror of a dream of prolonged female adolescence, innocent and dependent. When a man portrays lusty and aggressive older women as unnatural and evil, he is painting his envy of continued sexual vigor and his fear of losing his sexual dominance.

56. See Matthews' "The Wife of Bath" and Beltrán's "The Old Woman and Authority." The latter argues convincingly that the literary figure of the old woman as intermediary constitutes an attack against dualities basic to the foundation of the medieval universe, and that she "appears to be something of a hidden safety device (. . .) whose function is to keep the Western mind in contact with its body" (p.iv).

Editors' Introduction for Chapter II

[1]Stephen Gilman, *The Spain of Fernando de Rojas.* Princeton, New Jersey: Princeton University Press, 1972, pp. 160–165.

[2]James F. Calhoun, *et al., Abnormal Psychology,* second edition. CRM/Random House, 1977, p. 10.

Chapter II

1. Fernando de Rojas' the *Comedia de Calixto y Melibea* appeared in Burgos in 1499, in the dawn of the Spanish Renaissance. The printings in which most modern editions are based are the Burgos 1499, of sixteen acts or "actos"; Seville 1502, of twenty-one acts, which changed the title to *Tragicomedia de Calisto y Melibea;* and Valencia 1514, which brought the "actos" to their final number of twenty-two.

2. The place of magic in the *Celestina* has been the subject of animated controversy. Menendez y Pelayo saw clearly the importance of Celestina's bewitchment of Melibea for our understanding of the plot, but failed to fully understand the importance of the devil's intervention and of Celestina's role of *sorceress.* After Menendez y Pelayo *Celestina's* criticism only sporad-

ically has shown interest in its magic and diabolic aspects: in 1928 Julius Berzunza, in "Notes on Witchcraft and *Alcahuetería,*" *Romanic Review,* 19[1928]:141–150 studies the fate of witchcraft in the early Renaissance as well as the medical and magical properties of the remedies used by Celestina in her incantations. In 1932, F. Rauhut ("Das Dämonische in der Celestina," *Festgabe zum 60 Geburtstag Karl Vosslers* [Munich, 1932], pp. 117–148) concentrates on the philosophical significance of the devil's presence in *Celestina.* In 1952 José Bergamín, in a somewhat vague and loose essay, makes some assertions of merit: he insists on the importance of magic for our understanding of the *tragicomedia,* and of Celestina's *hilado* (yarn) as the instrument by which the devil is introduced as an active agent into the plot. But it is above all Peter Russell who has shown the importance of magic as a central theme of *La Celestina.* Professor Russell, in a few pages which condense immense erudition, points to the thematic core of the book, thus providing a fecund interpretative instrument placed against a background of magic and demonology; a whole world of images, a system of metaphors, suddenly acquire meaning and become, reciprocally, new tools for a deeper interpretation. Images of "yarn", "thread", "sewing", "spinning", "weaving", acquire, in this context, a meaning which confirms and enriches our knowledge of the book: P. E. Russell, "La magia como tema integral de la *Tragicomedia de Calisto y Melibea", (Studia Philológica, Homenaje ofrecido a Damaso Alonso,* 3[1963]; 337–54); rewritten and expanded, this article has appeared again in his book *Temas de la Celestina* (Madrid: Ariel, 1978), pp. 241–276. More recent studies are: Fernando Toro-Garland's "Celestina, hechicera clásica y tradicional", *Cuadernos Hispano Americanos,* 180 (1964), 438–445, which makes of the character of "hechicera" of Celestina a rhetorical device of "verisimilitude", since the *alcahuetas* were expected to be witches, and Elisabeth Sanchez' "Magic in *La Celestina", Hispanic Review,* 46 (1978); 481–484, which examines the tension between natural and supernatural explanations in the book, and concludes that the aim of magic is to point out the collapse of traditional morality and the need to turn to Christ.

3. A very useful book for our understanding of the place of magic in late 15th-century society is the *Malleus Maleficarum* ("Witch's Hammer"), written by the Inquisitors Henry Kramer and Fr. James Sprenger, who were greatly influential in the issuing of the Apostolic Bull *Summis desiderantes affectibus* on 9 December 1484, by Innocent VIII, and in the persecutions which followed it. I have used the *Malleus Maleficarum,* ed. Rev. Montague Summers (New York: Benjamin Bloom, 1970).

4. This seems to imply a kind of division of labor: the devil tempts the spirit and the witches the senses. This, however, is not strictly true, since the devil as well as the witches can induce *philocaptio* (irresistible love).

5. *Malleus,* p. 47. It is because of this supposed innate perversity of women that the general condemnation is against witches and not against wizards: see *Malleus,* pp. 41–48.

6. See *Malleus,* Part II, Question 1. "Of the Way Whereby a Formal Pact with Evil is Made", pp. 99–104.

7. *Malleus,* "Introduction", pp. xxxiv–xxxv.

8. The numbers of early editions show that the *Malleus* had an extraordinary diffusion, especially for a fifteenth-century book.

9. Celestina seems to have been a *sorceress* more than a *witch,* that is to say, to have used witchcraft for the furthering of her aims as a go-between more than for devotion to the devil. However, since the distinction is less clear in English, and since Mabbe's translation consistently uses "witch", I shall also do so. See *Russell,* note 15, pp. 272.

10. For the English translations I use *Celestina or the Tragicomedy of Calisto and Melibea,* translated from the Spanish by James Mabbe, anno 1631 (London: Routledge, 1923). Unfortunately Mabbe has either suppressed or glossed over all the obscene and irreverent references in the book, which are numerous. In these occasions I have rewritten the translation; I indicate in the notes when that is the case. The quotation in the text is *Mabbe,* pp. 20–21. [Note: the translations have been slightly modernized and Americanized—Eds.]

11. *Mabbe,* p. 26. Mabbe has given a wrong translation for *labrandera;* it means "seamstress" and not "laundress". This is a very serious mistake that destroys the metaphoric structure of the book.

12. I rewrite *Mabbe,* p. 27; Mabbe has suppressed all religious references. For the Spanish original I use *La Celestina La comedia [o trajicomedia] de Calisto i Melibea.* Manuel Criado de Val (Madrid: Editora Nacional, 1977); for the text quoted see pp. 74–75.

13. I have again rewritten *Mabbe,* p. 27; see *Criado de Val,* p. 75.

14. Mabbe had managed to change the totally irreverent sense of this paragraph: see *Mabbe,* p. 151 and *Criado de Val,* pp. 169–170.

15. To Celestina's "Mal sosegadilla deves tener la punta de la barriga" Mabbe gives the prudish translation "No motions at all to make in Venus' court?", See *Mabbe,* p. 34; *Criado de val,* p. 80.

16. *Mabbe,* p. 42 and *Criado de Val,* p. 86.

17. See *Criado de Val,* p. 146; Mabbe, of course, has suppressed all direct allusions to Areusa's body.

18. I translated directly from *Criado de Val* pp. 150–151 since Mabbe had refined the text out of existence.

19. My translation: see *Criado de Val,* p. 163.

20. My translation: see *Criado de Val,* p. 167.

21. *Russell,* p. 254.

22. *Malleus,* p. 170.

23. *Malleus,* p. 51.

24. Sebastián Cirac Estopañán, *Los procesos de hechicerías en la Inquisición de Castilla la Nueva* (Madrid: C.S.I.C., 1942), p. 105.

25. *Russell,* p. 260.

26. *Criado de Val,* p. 99.

27. Maurice Blanchot, *Lautréamont et Sade* (Paris: Minuit, 1953), p. 19. My translation.

Chapter III

1. Pierre Villey, *Les Sources et l'évolution des essais de Montaigne* (Paris: Hachette, 1908), 2 vols. II, 499–517.

2. Donald Frame, *Montaigne's Discovery of Man: The Humanization of a Humanist* (New York: Columbia University Press, 1955), p. 140.

3. Erik H. Erikson, *Identity and the Life Cycle: Selected Papers* (New York: *Psychological Issues,* I, 1959).

4. Montaigne was born in 1533. In 1571 he retired from his legal and diplomatic career to write. He published Books I and II of the *Essais* in 1580. He revised these extensively during the 1580's and added a third book in 1588. Until his death in 1592, he made numerous further additions to all three books. He rarely deleted his earlier views; instead, he created a mosaic of impressions from various periods of composition. Following tradition, I shall refer to passages written from 1571 to 1580 as "A-version"; to passages written from 1580 to 1588 as "B-version" or "B-addition"; and to passages written from 1588 to 1592 as "C-version" or "C-addition." All passages quoted are C-version unless otherwise noted. Translations are mine. The edition used is the Pléiade (Paris: Gallimard, 1961), edited by Albert Thibaudet. I refer to a French edition because translations do not indicate the different dates of composition of individual passages.

5. "Our feelings carry beyond us" (I, 3); "On the education of children" (I, 26); "On the affection fathers feel for their children" (II, 8); "Apologia for Raymond Sebond" (II, 12); "On presumption" (II, 17); "Concerning a monstrous child" (II, 30); "On repentance" (III, 2); "On vanity" (III, 9); "On experience" (III, 13).

6. See Frederick Rider, *The Dialectic of Selfhood in Montaigne* (Stanford, California: Stanford University Press, 1973), p. 30.

7. The few C-additions to I, 57, "De l'Age," also move away from solidarity, showing that aging has become more a personal than a humanistic concern.

8. See Marcel Gutwirth, *Michel de Montaigne ou le pari d'exemplarité* (Montreal, Quebec: Montreal University Press, 1977), p. 45.

Chapter IV

1. Derek Traversi, *An Approach to Shakespeare,* 3rd ed. (London: Hollis & Carter, 1968), Vol. 2, p. 147. It could just as well be argued that had he remained in power until he died or declared one of his daughters or sons-in-law to be Queen or King, he would have also encouraged anarchy or civil war.

2. Bernice Neugarten sees aging as a process of adaptation in which personality is the key element. Personality is pivotal in predicting which individuals will age successfully. See Bernice L. Neugarten, "Personality and Aging," in James E. Birren and K. Warner Schaie (eds.), *Handbook of the Psychology of Aging* (New York: Van Nostrand, 1977), p. 643.

3. G. B. Harrison (ed.) *Shakespeare: The Complete Works* (New York: Harcourt, Brace & World, Inc., 1968), p. 1138.

4. Traversi, p. 143.

5. Although some commentators have suggested that Edgar is cruelly getting back at his own father through Lear, it is more likely, in the context of the play as a whole, that he is acting in the role of a facilitator here, helping Lear to express his anger through fantasy. Twice he saves Gloucester, his father, from committing suicide.

Chapter V

1. For a survey of claims of extreme old age, see M. D. Grmek, *On Ageing and Old Age* (The Hague: W. Junk, 1958), pp. 33–37.

2. Leonard Hayflick, "The Biology of Human Aging," *The American Journal of the Medical Sciences,* 265 (1973), p. 437.

3. *La Comédie humaine,* edited by Pierre-Georges Castex (Paris: Gallimard, 1979), XII, 308. All references to Balzac's works will be to this edition unless otherwise stated. Subsequent references will be given in the text and will consist of a volume number in Roman numerals and a page number in Arabic numerals. Translations are my own.

4. *Le Centenaire* (Paris: Pollet, 1822), IV, 187.

Chapter VI

1. Page references below refer to these editions: *"Poor People" and "A Little Hero"* (New York: Doubleday, 1968); "Uncle's Dream" in *The Short Novels of Dostoevsky* (New York: Dial, 1958), pp. 225–342; *The Insulted and the Injured* (New York: Macmillan, 1923); "The Gambler" in *The Short Novels,* pp. 1–126; *Crime and Punishment* (New York: Norton, 1964); *A Raw Youth* (New York: Macmillan, 1956); and *The Brothers Karamazov* (New York: Harper and Brothers, 1960).

2. Letter to M. P. Fyodorov, 1873, quoted by Konstantin Mochulsky, *Dostoevsky: His Life and Work* (Princeton, N.J.: Princeton University Press, 1967), p. 169.

3. See Albert J. Guérard, *The Triumph of the Novel: Dickens, Dostoevsky, Faulkner* (New York: Oxford University Press, 1976), chapter 4, "Forbidden Games (II): Dostoevsky's Pedophilia," pp. 88–108. Dostoevsky sketched an account of a man's rape of his foster-sister in the notebooks for *The Idiot,* but then suppressed the episode.

4. For a discussion of defensive identity shifts in fiction, see Laurence M. Porter, "The Forbidden City: A Psychoanalytical Interpretation of Nodier's *Smarra,*" *Symposium,* 26, iv (Winter 1972: Special Issue on Psychoanalytic Approaches to Literary Texts): 331–348.

5. See Mochulsky, pp. 206–209.

6. This question was suggested to Dostoevsky by Balzac's *Le Père Goriot,* where two impecunious students discuss whether they would kill an old Mandarin in China—painlessly, effortlessly, and undetected—if they could therby enrich themselves. Dostoevsky's indignation at the sufferings of innocent children later inspired Albert Camus in *La Peste (The Plague).*

7. To be sure, Dostoevsky's depiction of female characters can be extreme in its anticipation of aging: a woman of twenty-eight is "no longer young" (*The Insulted and the Injured,* p. 220), and a woman of forty-three has already entered "old age" (*Crime and Punishment,* p. 197).

8. See Linda J. Ivanits, "Hagiography in *Brat'ja Karamazovy:* Zosima [sic], Ferapont, and the Russian Monastic Saint," *Russian Language Journal,* 34, no. 117 (Winter 1980): 109–126.

9. Gilbert D. Chaitin, "Religion as Defense: The Structure of *The Brothers Karamazov,*" *Literature and Psychology,* 22, ii (1972): 69–87 (pp. 75–77).

Editors' Introduction for Chapter VII

1. See Robert N. Butler, "The Life Review: An Interpretation of Reminiscence in the Aged," *Psychiatry,* 26 (1963), pp. 65–76; Robert N. Butler, "Looking Forward to What? The Life Review, Legacy and Excessive Identity Versus Change," *American Behavioral Scientist,* 14 (1970): 121–128; Myrna I. Lewis and Robert N. Butler, "Life Review Therapy," *Geriatrics,* 29 (1974): 165–173; and Robert N. Butler, *Why Survive? Being Old in America* (New York: Harper Colophon Books, 1976). The last work cited won a Pulitzer Prize. Some examples of the life review in film and fiction are cited in it, pp. 413–414.

Chapter VII

1. Marcel Proust. *A la recherche du temps perdu.* Paris: Bibliothèque de la Pléiade, 1954. Volume III, p. 907. All quotations come from this same volume, and only the page number will be given in parentheses henceforth. All translations are mine.

Chapter VIII

1. Yasuichi Awakawa, *Zen Painting* (Tokyo: Kodansha International, 1970), p. 28. Editions used for this chapter are: Yasunari Kawabata, *The Master of Go* (New York: Berkley Pub. Corps., 1974), and *The Sound of the Mountain* (Tokyo: Charles E. Tuttle and Co., 1977), both translated by Edward G. Seidensticker.
2. Awakawa, p. 23.
3. Analogies between the Westerner's notion of the game may be made with Mallarmé and his dice throw; Pushkin's *Queen of Spades,* and more.

Editors' Introduction for Chapter IX

1. On character types, see Robert E. Scholes and Robert Kellogg, *The Nature of Narrative* (New York: Oxford University Press, 1966).
2. On the fairy-tale as moral teaching, see Bruno Bettelheim, *The Uses of Enchantment: The Meaning and Importance of Fairy Tales* (New York: Random House, 1976).

Chapter IX

1. Eudora Welty, "The Worn Path," *A Curtain of Green and Other Stories* (New York: Harcourt Brace, 1941), p. 276; p. 280.
2. "Is Phoenix Jackson's Grandson Really Dead?" *Critical Inquiry,* 1 (September, 1974), 220.
3. Ibid., p. 221.
4. Alexander Solzhenitsyn, "Matryona's House," tr. Michael Glenny, *Ten Classics of Modern Fiction,* ed. Irving Howe (New York: Harcourt Brace, 1968), p. 637.

5. See Irving Howe, Introduction to "Matryona's House", *Ten Classics. . . .* p. 619.
6. G. M. Trevelyan, *History of England,* Vol. III (Garden City: Doubleday Anchor, 1952), p. 193.
7. Anthony Trollope, *The Warden and Barchester Towers* (Boston: Houghton Mifflin, 1966), p. 510.
8. Honoré de Balzac, *Old Goriot,* tr. Marion Ayton Crawford (London: Penguin, 1951), p. 50.
9. Frank Norris, *McTeague* (New York: Fawcett, 1960), p. 32.
10. Such a contrapuntal use of an old person with a single quirky habit is by no means unique. Ibsen has his old Ekdal in *The Wild Duck,* a man whose obsession with an attic "hunting park" turns out to be far more benign than the self-aggrandizing illusions of his son Hjalmar or the zealous obsession with "truth" of the god-playing Gregers. In *The Plague* Camus has his old Spanish asthmatic who plies his time passing dried peas from one vessel to another, but attains more saintliness than the driven Tarrou, who consciously dedicated himself to secular anointment. In all of these cases, of course, one must suspect a dash of irony in the sanctification of a private quirkiness that is both aimless and passive; yet the static activity of an old person becomes that appropriate nonteleological counterweight for the misguided *telos* that is the real satiric target.
11. Anton Chekhov, *The Cherry Orchard,* tr. Tyrone Guthrie and Leonid Kipnis (Minneapolis: University of Minnesota Press, 1965), p. 70.
12. Bernard Shaw, *Heartbreak House,* (London: Penguin, 1964), p. 128.
13. Arnold Bennett, *The Old Wives' Tale* (London: Thos. Nelson, 1908), p. 600.
14. Tillie Olsen, "Tell Me A Riddle," *Tell Me A Riddle, A Collection by Tillie Olsen* (Philadelphia and New York: Lippincott, 1961), p. 98.
15. Updike's *The Poorhouse Fair* comes close to presenting an entirely geriatric cast, but its core character is the utopian Conner, who is always presented in counterpoint with the elderly residents of the home he directs.
16. Muriel Spark, *Memento Mori* (Philadelphia and New York: Lippincott, 1959), p. 222.
17. The old couple's suicide parallels a primitive folk tradition found in the Fiji Islands and some Indian cultures. Another modern literary version is the suicide of Willy Loman in *Death of a Salesman.*
18. Eugene Ionesco, *The Chairs,* tr. Donald M. Allen, *Four Plays by Eugene Ionesco* (New York: Grove, 1958), p. 144.
19. Samuel Beckett, *Endgame* (New York: Grove, 1958), p. 1.
20. Ruby Cohn, "Endgame," *Twentieth-Century Interpretations of Endgame,* ed. Bell Gale Chevigny (Englewood Cliffs: Prentice Hall, 1969), p. 42.

SELECT BIBLIOGRAPHY

I. *Bibliographies of Works on Aging*

AGE IS BECOMING: AN ANNOTATED BIBLIOGRAPHY ON WOMEN AND AGING. Berkeley, CA: Interface Bibliographers, 1977. Sponsored by NOW. Integrates feminist issues with the problems of aging. Z 7164.0413/1977.

ALLYN, MILDRED V. About Aging. A Catalog of Films, 1979.4th ed. Los Angeles: Ethel Percy Andrus Gerontology Center, 1979. HQ 1064.US564/1979. Lists videocassettes, 457 16mm films, and 63 feature films. Annotations by the distributors; subject index.

ALVAREZ, RONALD A. F. and SUSAN C. KLINE. Self-Discovery in the Humanities II: Images of Aging in Literature. Washington, D.C.: National Council on the Aging 1978. Pp. 135.

FREEMAN, JOSEPH T. Aging, Its History and Literature. New York: Human Sciences Press, 1979. HQ1061.F713. Includes lists of writers on old age, and studies about them, from classical antiquity to the present, with an emphasis on Western Europe from the 16th through the 19th century.

GERONTOLOGY: A CROSS-NATIONAL CORE LIST OF SIGNIFICANT WORKS. Ann Arbor: Institute of Gerontology, The University of Michigan: 1982. Z 7164.04E83/1982. Supersedes *Gerontology: A Core List of Significant Works* (1978). Covers Canada, the United Kingdom, and the United States, with some reference to other countries and to cross-national studies. Compiled by an eighty-four-member international panel. Lists about 2,300 titles without comment. 8 reference categories and 33 subject categories. Includes essays on historical developments in gerontology.

MOSS, WALTER. G., et al., eds. Humanistic Perspectives on Aging: An Annotated Bibliography and Essay. Ann Arbor: Institute of Gerontology, 1976. 2nd ed. Lists non-fiction, autobiographies, fiction, reflections on death, and films and videotapes, with useful descriptive commentary. Other bibliographies on aging are also available through the Institute of Gerontology, 520 E. Liberty, Ann Arbor, MI 48109.

MUELLER, J. E. et al. "Bibliography of Doctoral Dissertations on Aging from American Institutions of Higher Learning (1954–)," appearing in July issues of *The Journal of Gerontology* beginning with 1971.

PLACE, LINNA FUNK, et al. Aging and the Aged: An Annotated Bibliography and Library Resource Guide. Boulder: Westview Press, 1981. Z 7164.04P52. Excellent annotations which by themselves provide a useful introductory overview.

II. *Studies of Aging in Literature*

ALBRIGHT, DANIEL. The Myth against Myth: A Study of Yeat's Imagination in Old Age. London: Oxford University Press, 1972. PR 5907.A85. A complex study of how Yeats in his late poetry accepts the role of a watcher, renounces the hope of immortality, and says farewell to art.

BEAUVOIR, SIMONE DE. La Vieillesse. Paris: Gallimard, 1970. Translated variously as "The Coming of Age" (New York, NY: Putnam,

1972) and "Old Age." HV 1451.B413/1972.The vast compendium of material on aging is disappointing in its details. Literary works are treated superficially, and the volume is marred by inaccuracies.

BONDY, FRANÇOIS. "Italo Svevo and Ripe Old Age," *Hudson Review,* 20 (Winter 1967–68): 575–98. AP 2.H886. "More than all catastrophes—aging is the image of inexorable fate" which he transmutes into comedy.

ERIKSON, ERIK. "Reflections on Dr. Borg's Life Cycle," *Daedalus,* 105, ii (Spring 1976): 1–28. AS 36.D3. A famous study of the protagonist in Ingmar Bergman's film *Wild Strawberries,* an aging professor who belatedly recognizes his need and capacity for love.

THE GERONTOLOGIST has published many articles on aging in literature, usually denouncing unsympathetic attitudes.

KESTER, RUDOLF. "The Portrayal of Age in Hesse's Narrative Prose," *Germanic Review,* 41 (March 1966): 111–19. PD 1.G4. Traces his evolution from depicting "the psychic instability of age and its pathos" in the early works to presenting laconic Jungian archetypes of "The Wise Old Man" in later ones.

MIGNON, ELISABETH. Crabbed Age and Youth: The Old Men and Woman in the Restoration Comedy of Manners. Durham, North Carolina: Duke University Press, 1947. PR 698.04M5. Describes unflagging abuse of the elderly in English comedy between 1660 and 1700, in contrast to the sympathetic and varied treatments of them by Shakespeare, earlier, and by the sentimental 18th-century drama later. In the Restoration old age and comic vice were one. A cult of youth made men suddenly old at 30, women at 20.

NITECKI, ALICIA K. "The Convention of the Old Man's Lament in (Chaucer's) *Pardoner's Tale," The Chaucer Review,* 16 i (Summer, 1982): 76–84. PR 1901.C47. "By using the commonplace mimetically in the *Pardoner's Tale,* Chaucer opens it up to new psychological significance" as it expresses "longing for transcendence."

RICHARDSON, BESSIE ELLEN. Old Age Among the Ancient Greeks: The Greek Portrayal of Old Age in Literature, Art, and Inscriptions, With a Study of the Duration of Life among the Ancient Greeks on the Basis of Inscriptional Evidence. Baltimore: Johns Hopkins University Press, 1933. CC 21.J6 no.16. An exhaustive scholarly study, with a full bibliography of primary sources on pages 363–72.

SPICKER, STUART F., WOODWARD, KATHLEEN M., VAN TASSEL, DAVID D. Aging and the Elderly: Humanistic Perspectives in Gerontology. Atlantic Highlands, New Jersey: Humanities Press Inc., 1978. HQ 1061.A457.

WOODWARD, KATHLEEN M. At Last, the Real Distinguished Thing: The Late Poems of Eliot, Pound, Stevens, and Williams. Columbus: The Ohio State University Press, 1980. PS 310.A34W6. An important study which affirms the wisdom of old age as the culmination of personal growth. It involves "creative readiness for the unexpected moment, a receptivity to experience, which has been prepared by a long process of learning about the relationship between the self and the world, the mind and the world." Not passivity or stagnation, but stillness.

III. *Also of Interest*

ACHENBAUM, W. ANDREW. Old Age in the New Land: The American Experience since 1790. Baltimore: Johns Hopkins University Press, 1978. HQ 1064.U5A26. A thorough, scholarly analysis of how American society has seen and dealt with the aged.

THE AGE OF AGING: A READER IN SOCIAL GERONTOLOGY. Buffalo, NY: Prometheus Books, 1979. HQ 1064.U5A633. A sprightly anthology with considerable treatment of psychological aspects.

AGING IN CULTURE AND SOCIETY: COMPARATIVE VIEWPOINTS AND STRATEGIES. Christine L. Fry and Contributors. New York, NY: Prager, 1980. GN 485.A34. A fine example of how anthropology can and should deepen our understanding of aging, this text is also a nice introduction to the field of anthropology. The emphasis is on ethnology. "Myths are shattered."

BAUM, MARTHA, and RAINER C. BAUM. Growing Old: A Societal Perspective. Englewood Cliffs, N.J.: Prentice-Hall, 1980. HQ 1061.B38. An expert treatment.

BENET, SULA. Abkhasians. The Long-living People of the Caucasus. New York: Holt, Rinehart and Winston, Inc. 1974. DK 34.A2B46. This fascinating ethnography, a landmark in anthropological gerontology, looks at longevity in Soviet Georgia. "He cooperates rather than competes."

BLYTHE, RONALD. The View in Winter: Reflections on Old Age. New York: Harcourt Brace Jovanovich, 1979. HQ 1064.G7B58. Beautifully written, with reflections of old people interviewed by the author. The introduction has significant commentaries on aging in literature.

BUTLER, ROBERT N. "Successful Aging." *Mental Hygiene,* 58:3 (1974): 6–12. BF 173.A2M5. Examines myths of aging, elaborates on the life review, and refers to literary examples.

____________."The Life Review: An Interpretation of Reminiscence in the Aged." *Psychiatry,* 26 (1963): 65–76. RC 321.P9. An original psychotherapeutic approach is examined in this seminal article enriched with literary examples.

____________. Why Survive? Being Old in America. New York: Harper and Row, 1975. HQ 1064.U5.B87. The Pulitzer Prize-winning resource book makes use of devastating statistics and compelling examples. Sections on politics and policy remain timely under Reaganomics, and the muckraking comments on institutional psychiatry are frightening.

ERIKSON, ERIK H. Identity and the Life Cycle: Selected Papers. New York: W. W. Norton, 1980 (1959). BF 1.P78 v.1. An earlier version is included in his *Childhood and Society.* An epoch-making interpretation of old age, not in terms of relationships between the persons and the outside (disengagement theory or activity theory) but in terms of the relationship of the old person to him or herself. Human development continues throughout life; the task of the last stage is to avoid self-contempt and to achieve integrity. This means accepting the fact of death, but recognizing one's unique contribution to the series of generations.

FISCHER, DAVID HACKETT. Growing Old in America. NY: Oxford University Press, 1977. A thought-provoking historical study but with some problems in the data. Fischer looks at an elite population in Puritan New England, then tends to extrapolate to general aging in America. First and last sections are of greatest interest. HQ 1064.U5F5.

HANDBOOK OF AGING AND THE SOCIAL SCIENCES. New York: Van Nostrand Reinhold, 1976. Edited by Robert H. Binstock and Ethel Shanas. HQ 1061.H336. Comprehensive, scholarly and readable, a vast treasury of information with thousands of references to other works.

HANDBOOK OF THE PSYCHOLOGY OF AGING. New York: Van Nostrand Reinhold, 1977. Edited by James E. Birren and K. Warner Schaie. BF 724.8H36. Same commentary applies as for *Handbook* above.

HERR, J. J. and J. H. WEAKLAND. Counseling Elders and Their Families: Practical Techniques for Applied Gerontology. New York: Springer Publications, 1979. BF 724.8.H46. An exciting book, employing a skillful use of paradoxical techniques.

INTERNATIONAL HANDBOOK ON AGING: CONTEMPORARY DEVELOPMENTS AND RESEARCH. Westport: Greenwood Press, 1980. Ed. by Erdman Palmore, HQ 1061.I535/1980. Individual sections on 28 countries where significant work on gerontology is taking place. Eminent contributors. Extensive bibliographies. Treats demography, social services, needs, theory, and history.

KOCH, KENNETH. I Never Told Anybody: Teaching Poetry Writing in a Nursing Home. New York: Random House, 1977. PN 1101.K55. An extraordinary account of how a New York poet tapped the creativity and liveliness of some very old people, giving them a sense of mastery and fulfillment. The anthologized poems are often moving.

OLD AGE ON THE NEW SCENE. New York: Springer, 1981. Edited by Robert Kastenbaum. HQ 1061.039. A wide-ranging anthology of brief essays on aging and society, with bibliography.

OLD PEOPLE IN THREE INDUSTRIAL SOCIETIES. New York: Atherton Press, 1968. Edited by Ethel Shanas. HQ 1061.04. A solidly-documented comparative survey of health, social welfare, family and social structure, work and finances of the elderly in Denmark, Great Britain, and the United States.

PALMORE, ERDMAN BALLAGH. The Honorable Elders: A Cross-Cultural Analysis of Aging in Japan. Durham, NC: Duke University Press, 1975. HQ 1064.J3P34. Well-documented, shows a changing Japan with ambivalence toward the aged despite a strong remainder of traditional filial piety. Several short stories are mentioned in ch. 7.

PHILIBERT, MICHEL. "The Phenomenological Approach to Images of Aging." *Soundings,* No. 1 (Spring 1974): 33–49. BV 1460.C6. Makes a case for humanistic gerontology.

SOCIAL PROBLEMS OF THE AGING: READINGS. Mildred M. Seltzer, Sherry L. Corbett, Robert C. Atchley, eds. Belmont, California: Wadsworth Publishing Company, 1978. HQ 1064.45 S596. Good introduction to aging in America through previously published essays.

SOURCEBOOK ON AGING. Chicago: Marquis Academic Media, 1979. 2nd ed. HQ 1064.f.U5S68/1979. An anthology of materials on Health,

Retirement, Legislation, Statistic, and Resources, including many government publications, tables, and lists.

SOURCEBOOK ON DEATH AND DYING. Chicago: Marquis Professional Publications, 1982. HQ 1073.5fU6S68/1982. Includes a selection of articles published after 1976 on Euthanasia, Patient Rights, Bereavement Counseling, Funerals, Hospice Programs, Financial and Legal Issues. Extensive bibliography; directory of self-help groups.

STEARNS, PETER. Old Age in European Society: The Case of France. New York, NY: Holmes and Meier, 1976. HQ 1064.F7S73/1976. An interesting historical account.

TEICHER, MORTON I., DANIEL THURSZ, and JOSEPH L. VIGILANTE. Reaching the Aged. Social Services in Forty-Four Countries. Beverly Hills: SAGE Publications, 1979. HV 1451.R4. This international effort contributes new perspectives to our understanding of services to the aged. Countries studied include Poland, South Africa, Israel, China, and Yugoslavia.

TROLL, LILLIAN; MILLER, SHEILA and ATCHLEY, ROBERT. Families in Later Life. Belmont, California: Wadsworth, 1978. HQ 536.T67. Useful look at the impact of aging on family systems.

VAN TASSEL, DAVID, ed. *Aging, Death and the Completion of Being*. Philadelphia: University of Pennsylvania Press, 1979. HQ 1061.A4575. Contains essays on literature by Leon Edel, Leslie Fiedler and others.

INDEX of WORKS CITED